A Britespot Publication

NORMAN WHITESIDE

My Memories of Man Utd

Bryan Robson, the best player that I've ever played alongside

FOREWORD

Bryan Robson OBE

Today, the name of Norman Whiteside still conjures up memories of epic encounters from Manchester United's history, as well as that of a battling midfielder creating havoc across Old Trafford and beyond, giving his all for the famous red shirt.

It also conjures up a figure of hate in the eyes of supporters of other clubs and sends a shudder down the spine of opposition players, fearful of his reputed reputation.

It was a reputation, at times completely unfounded, with a boyish enthusiasm and a dedicated will to win more the cause of his on field actions rather than the thuggish mentality that many associated him with.

Throughout the history of Manchester United Football Club there have been many figures who have been accorded legendary status, names such as Billy Meredith, Johnny Carey, Duncan Edwards, Denis Law, Bobby Charlton, George Best, Eric Cantona, Roy Keane, Ryan Giggs and David Beckham are but a few of those. Norman Whiteside is another and is certainly not out of place alongside those others.

Those who followed United in the 1980's took Norman to their hearts, encouraging every tackle and cheering every goal. He had come up through the youth system, as had Edwards, Colman, Best etc. His mistakes were forgiven, his faults went unseen. He was United through and through.

For me, Norman Whiteside conjures up three images. The first is Norman at his best against Liverpool at Anfield in April 1988. The second is his goal against Arsenal at Villa Park in the FA Cup semi-final of 1983. The third is another goal, this time on a very warm Saturday afternoon at Wembley in 1985, when his curling shot past Neville Southall secured the FA Cup for us.

For me personally it was an honour to play alongside Norman in the red of Manchester United.

This book contains those three memorable moments along with many others, which will warm the heart and recall the career of one of Manchester United's greatest and most popular players – Norman Whiteside.

Me with a dodgy haircut!

Norman Whiteside My Memories of Man Utd
A Britespot Publication

First Published in Great Britain by
Britespot Publishing Solutions Limited
Chester Road, Cradley Heath, West Midlands B64 6AB

ISBN 1 904103 21 9

Cover design and layout
© *Britespot Publishing Solutions Limited*

Norman Whiteside Acknowledgments:
I would like to thank all the following people in no particular order:

My family for all their support over the years including my Ma Aileen and Da Norman.
My brother's Ken and Hughie. My children Della, Blaine and Clodagh and their mother Julie.

Eddie Cooke of the 72nd Battalion Boys Brigade. Norman Davis, the best kitman in the world. Jim McGregor the physio with the healing touch. Teresa at The Cliff training ground for cooking all that delicious food. Nicky Welch for putting a shine back in my boots. Bob Bishop who sent me to Old Trafford. Bet and Tom Fannon, my landlord and lady in the early days. Michael Prophet, a wonderful hotelier and even better friend and Pete 'Sleepy' Clavin the Stockbroker.

The Managers and Coaches who have influenced my career including Ron Atkinson, Billy Bingham, Sir Alex Ferguson, Colin Harvey, Howard Kendall, Dave Sexton, Syd Owen, Eric Harrison and Jimmy Curran. My early days at school including Willy 'Oxo' Williamson, Herbie 'Honey' Artt, Victor 'The Coalman' Anderson.

My drinking buddies Robbo, Big Paul and those I can't remember!

My close colleague Viv Anderson. My confidant and friend Geoff and all of my friends too many to mention by name.

From Britespot Publishing: Roger Marshall, Paul Burns, Chris Sweet, Darren Cartwright, Chris Russell and Linda Perkins.

Last but not least 'Moet' Manson.

Publisher Acknowledgments:
The publisher would like to thank Norman Whiteside. Jim Cadman for the inception of the 'My Memories' series. Jackie Cutting, Pauline Walker and Ian Nannestad. Jen Little of Empics and Andy Cowie of Colorsport.

Finally, Iain McCartney who, without his contribution, this book would not have been possible.

Photos © Empics and Colorsport

Lifting the FA Cup with team-mate Kevin Moran who had an early bath

CONTENTS
Chapters   Page

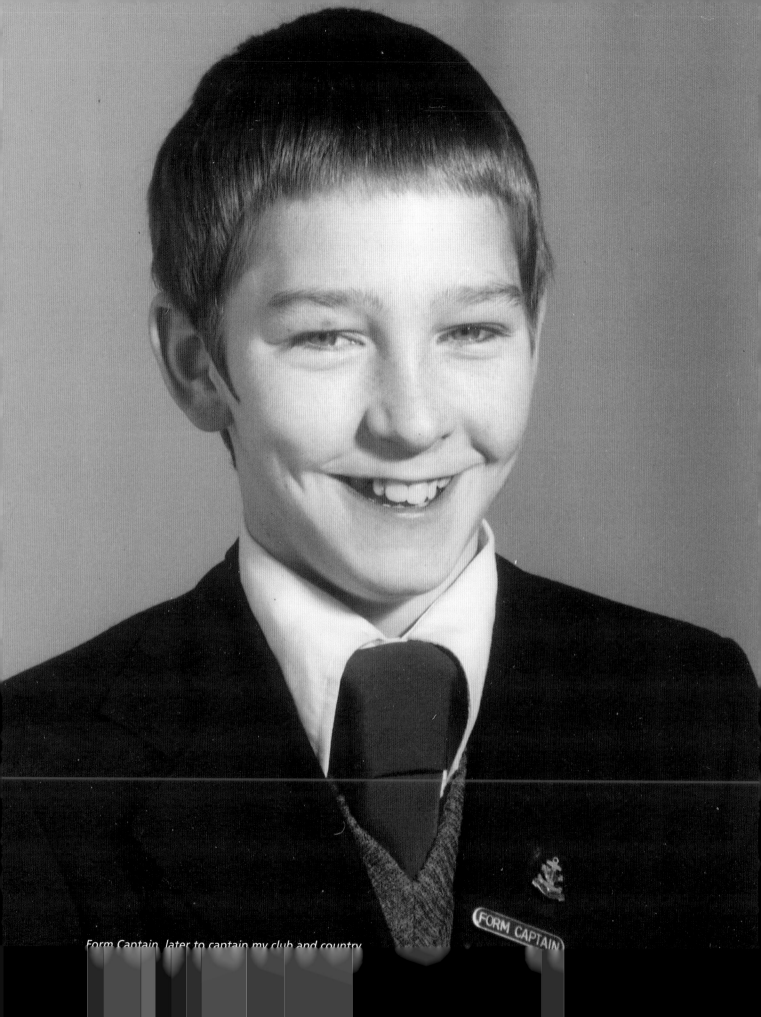

Form Captain, later to captain my club and country.

Chapter 1

THE BELFAST BOY
The Beginning of a Legend

For many, the mere mention of Belfast's Shankhill Road sends a shiver down the spine and conjures up pictures of an area beset with some of the worst sectarian violence seen in the city. For others, like myself, who went about our lives the best we could, trying to ignore the goings on around us, it was home.

Ignoring everyday outbreaks of violence and the sounds of distant explosions was difficult, but football helped to take your mind off things.

There is no denying that it was a hard area to grow up in, but it was where we lived, so we simply got on with it. I came from a working-class background and I managed to find something of an escape route through football. Something that many of the lads I knew from school were unable to do.

One of the other major problems besides the sectarianism was that there was not really that much to do, so football had a double use. On one hand it kept me away from the troubles and on the other, gave me an outlet for my boyish enthusiasm.

"United chief scout Joe Brown came over to Belfast to see me, and as a fourteen year old I signed schoolboy forms for Manchester United"

As a seven-year-old, I began playing for the 72nd Battalion of the Boys Brigade, where I experienced organised football for the first time. Occasionally, I managed to hit double figures during a game, but if I did manage to score ten, I was more than often moved back into defence to give both the opposition and our other forwards a chance.

I can remember one game in a tournament at Blackpool in 1975 against Lytham St Annes, when I scored a hat-trick in the opening five minutes. The Brigade officers were so embarrassed, that they made up some excuse that I was injured or something and took me off. The following day, I went out and scored six against the Manchester Battalion.

Looking back, I must have gave some of the opposition something to think about even before I had kicked a ball, as I was a bit taller than many of them and had a wicked 'skinhead' haircut. This was nothing to do with projecting a 'hard man' image, but mainly for hygienic reasons, as I worked as a coal lorry helper to earn some pocket money and the coal dust was very hard to shift.

School for me was Cairnmartin Secondary where I managed to score around one hundred goals in one season and at the age of twelve, I was playing for the Northern Ireland schoolboy side. Two years later, I was still there and had been elevated to captain. I was also captain of the school side when we won three trophies in 1980, a year that saw me score six times in the replayed school's Cup Final.

One particular match I can always remember, saw the opposition coach screaming at his defenders to close me down and prevent me from getting the ball on my favoured left foot. Determined to silence the voice on the touch line, I received a pass some twenty-five yards out, switched it to my right foot and struck it firmly past the goalkeeper. The tactical advice to the opposition came to a halt.

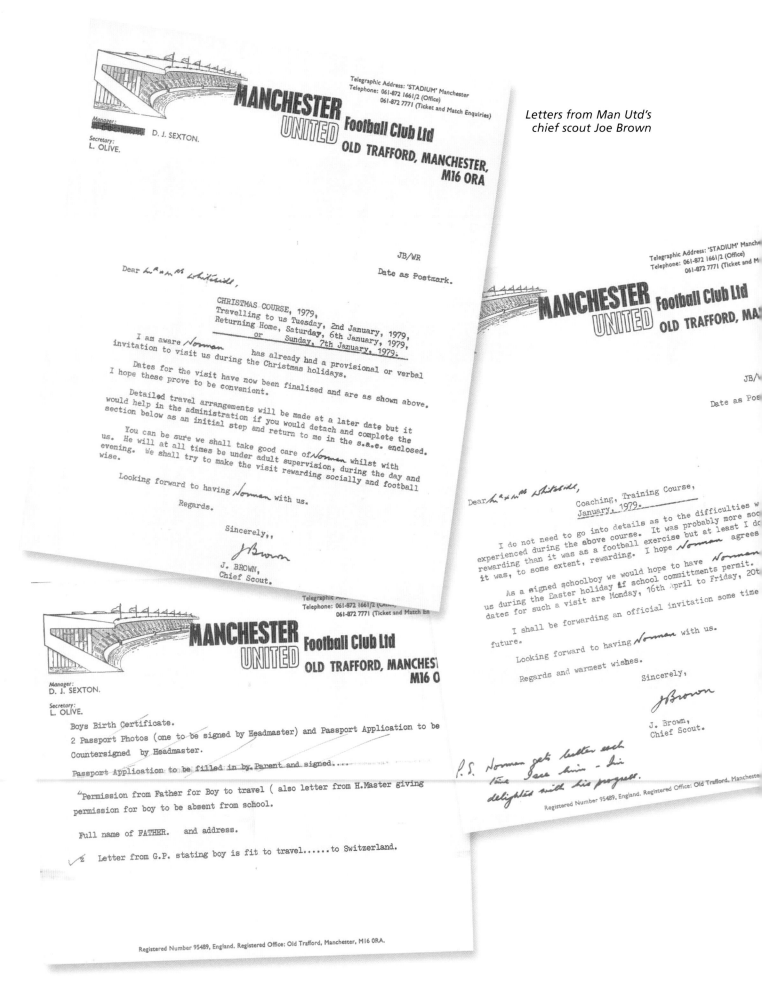

Letters from Man Utd's chief scout Joe Brown

Letter 1 (top left):

Manager:
D. J. SEXTON.

Secretary:
L. OLIVE.

MANCHESTER UNITED Football Club Ltd
OLD TRAFFORD, MANCHESTER, M16 ORA

Telegraphic Address: 'STADIUM' Manchester
Telephone: 061-872 1661/2 (Office)
061-872 7771 (Ticket and Match Enquiries)

JB/WR

Date as Postmark.

Dear *Mr & Mrs Whiteside*,

CHRISTMAS COURSE, 1979,
Travelling to us Tuesday, 2nd January, 1979,
Returning Home, Saturday, 6th January, 1979,
or Sunday, 7th January, 1979.

I am aware *Norman* has already had a provisional or verbal invitation to visit us during the Christmas holidays.

Dates for the visit have now been finalised and are as shown above. I hope these prove to be convenient.

Detailed travel arrangements will be made at a later date but it would help in the administration if you would detach and complete the section below as an initial step and return to me in the s.a.e. enclosed.

You can be sure we shall take good care of *Norman* whilst with us. He will at all times be under adult supervision, during the day and evening. We shall try to make the visit rewarding socially and football wise.

Looking forward to having *Norman* with us.

Regards.

Sincerely,

J. Brown

J. BROWN,
Chief Scout.

Letter 2 (right):

Telegraphic Address: 'STADIUM' Manchester
Telephone: 061-872 1661/2 (Office)
061-872 7771 (Ticket and M...

MANCHESTER UNITED Football Club Ltd
OLD TRAFFORD, MA...

JB/W...

Date as Pos...

Dear *Mr & Mrs Whiteside*,

Coaching, Training Course,
January, 1979.

I do not need to go into details as to the difficulties w... experienced during the above course. It was probably more soo... rewarding than it was as a football exercise but at least I do... it was, to some extent, rewarding. I hope *Norman* agrees...

As a signed schoolboy we would hope to have *Norman*... us during the Easter holiday if school committments permit... dates for such a visit are Monday, 16th April to Friday, 20t...

I shall be forwarding an official invitation some time... future.

Looking forward to having *Norman* with us.

Regards and warmest wishes.

Sincerely,

J. Brown

J. Brown,
Chief Scout.

P.S. *Norman gets better each time I see him - his... delighted with his progress.*

Registered Number 95489, England. Registered Office: Old Trafford, Manchester...

Letter 3 (bottom left):

Manager:
D. J. SEXTON.

Secretary:
L. OLIVE.

MANCHESTER UNITED Football Club Ltd
OLD TRAFFORD, MANCHEST...
M16 O...

Telegraphic Ad...
Telephone: 061-872 1661/2 (Offi...
061-872 7771 (Ticket and Match En...

Boys Birth Certificate.

2 Passport Photos (one to be signed by Headmaster) and Passport Application to be Countersigned by Headmaster.

Passport Application to be filled in by Parent and signed.....

"Permission from Father for Boy to travel (also letter from H.Master giving permission for boy to be absent from school.

Full name of FATHER. and address.

Letter from G.P. stating boy is fit to travel......to Switzerland.

Registered Number 95489, England. Registered Office: Old Trafford, Manchester, M16 ORA.

As a schoolboy, I also played for the Belfast branch of the Liverpool Supporters Club. Honest! If only they knew then that I was destined to play for their dreaded rivals and how I would perform against their club in the years to come then I am certain that they would never have allowed me within a hundred yards of them.

Schoolboy football in the 1970's is incomparable to that of the present day. The enthusiasm of the players and those who give up their time at this grass roots level of the game remain the same, but organised football is now more widely available for boys (and girls) from a much younger age. Media coverage has also altered greatly, with all levels of football widely covered on television and in print.

So, it is perhaps strange that back in April 1979, one of the national dailies, not some regional rag from the back of beyond, dedicated half a page to yours truly, then a thirteen-year-old schoolboy. They also went as far as to include a photograph! Many I am sure would have passed the article over if it had not been for the eight word heading in bold print which accompanied the article 'Have United Found The New Best At Last?' The dye was set.

Derek Allsop (The Daily Mail)
"Norman Whiteside looked like a US Marine due to his hair cut. His long legs take him on a meandering course rather than the jinking run which simplified Best. There is, however, one important common denominator – the nerve to produce the goals on the big occasion."

The article had appeared following an international youth tournament at Manchester City's Maine Road, when I had contributed to Northern Ireland's 2-1 win over Wales by scoring the first and making the second. The only thing that I remember saying to the reporter was that I wanted to play for Manchester United. This was not just some wild ambition that I held, but one that had already seen the seeds sown, as United had already made an approach to me and it was where my future belonged.

It was also around this time that the initial interest in my play began to transpire, with Ipswich Town one of the first club's to do so. In fact, they went as far as to approach me, but there was only one team I wanted to play for and I decided to hold off in the hope that they would eventually come for me.

> "Ignoring everyday outbreaks of violence
> and the sounds of distant explosions was difficult,
> but football helped to take your mind off things"

Having been originally spotted by Bob Bishop, the man whose vision had pushed George Best across the Irish Sea to Manchester over a decade earlier, the United chief scout Joe Brown came over to Belfast to see me, and as a fourteen year old I signed schoolboy forms for Manchester United.

Obviously, I was still at school and had to continue with my studies, which were now of secondary importance to me. The club did ask me if I was interested in moving to Manchester, but this did not immediately appeal to me and I was allowed to stay in Belfast and travel over when required. Perhaps the club was slightly wary as a result of the circumstances surrounding George Best's initial journey in the same direction.

My Ma and Da
Aileen and Norman

Anyway, it was arranged that I could travel over for weekend games and I soon became more familiar with the Belfast to Manchester shuttle than the local bus service. I would travel over on the Friday night after school and return twenty-four hours later. Eventually the weekend commuting came to an end and I had to leave Belfast to take up residence in Manchester.

After a while it wasn't only weekends that I travelled across the Irish Sea, as I was sometimes flown for mid week fixtures. One of those first trips was for my debut in the United youth team against Derby County on January 26th 1981 in a fourth round F.A. Youth Cup tie. Suspension to David Wynn allowed me to play at inside right in a game that ended in a 1-1 draw. I kept my place for the replay on February 2nd, moving to inside left.

I was also flown over to London for the FA Youth Cup semi-final against Tottenham Hotspur at White Hart Lane. I was one of two schoolboys in the side, the other being John Armfield, son of the former Blackpool and England full back. At full time he was driven back to the Lancashire resort, while I was flown home, so that we could attend school the following day.

"I must have gave some of the opposition something to think about, as I was a bit taller than many of them and had a wicked 'skinhead' haircut"

We lost that particular match 3-0 and I can remember picking up a calf injury in a rather physical encounter. It was not, however, quite as physical as the second leg, when Spurs had five players booked as they fought their way into the final on a 3-1 aggregate in front of a 2,101 crowd.

Prior to the start of season 1980-81, I made my first appearance at Old Trafford and I am sure that many, if not most, of the crowd in attendance at the club open day, which was held in aid of charity, had no idea who I was.

The highlight of the afternoon's entertainment was an "international six-a-side competition", with the teams made up from the United first-team squad. I was there simply to make up the numbers for the Northern Ireland team, lining up alongside Sammy McIlroy, Tom Sloan, Jimmy Nicholl, Chris McGrath and Tom Connell. As luck would have it, we made the final (after beating 'England'), where we defeated the 'Rest of the World' side 4-1. Chris McGrath scored twice, Jimmy Nicholl and myself snatching the others. Not bad for a mere schoolboy!

As an associate schoolboy, I began my United career on the bottom rung, playing in the 'A' and 'B' teams, with The Cliff training ground as our 'home'. Often I found myself not only playing against boys who were a bit older than myself, but also up against seasoned professionals with Football League experience. Fortunately, I never felt out of my depth and playing against those older and more experienced opponents helped me prepare for the years ahead.

United, as they did for all their youngsters found me accommodation and I went to stay with Beth and Thomas Fannon in Chorlton-cum-Hardy. It did not take long to settle and I was not on my own in the strange surroundings, as Kevin Moran and Ashley Grimes were also under Mrs Fannon's wing, with Paul McGrath arriving later. I fitted in easy enough and caused Beth very few, if any, problems, as both she and her husband were very easy to get along with.

*Thinking about
my future career*

Beth Fannon (Norman's Landlady in Manchester)
"When Norman left school he came to live with us and he was no trouble to look after. When I first saw him, however, I was surprised by his size for someone of his age. He kept his room tidy enough and liked his food. The boys had a curfew of 10.30pm, except for a Saturday night when they could stay out later. Then, they would often watch Match of the Day before heading out to a club that was mainly for teenagers. I would never hear them creep in a few hours later."

"Have United Found The New Best At Last? read the heading to a half page article dedicated to yours truly - back in April 1979"

The club very seldom checked up on us, but I am sure Mrs Fannon kept them up to date. We were allowed to eat more or less what we wanted and quite often after Paul McGrath arrived, we would go out for a Chinese.

Despite my United career taking off smoothly, season 1981-82 came to a disappointing end, as it saw me having to go into hospital for a cartilage operation, which forced me to miss out a little in the pre-season training and worse of all the start of the following season itself.

MANCHESTER UNITED Football Club Ltd

OLD TRAFFORD, MANCHESTER, M16 ORA

Manager:
R. ATKINSON.

Secretary:
L. OLIVE.

	£	250.	per week basic wages	29/12/82 – 31/7/84
	£	300.	per week basic wages	1/8/84 – 31/7/85
	£	350.	per week basic wages	1/8/85 – 31/7/86
1.	£	400.	**per week basic wage.**	1/8/86 – 31/7/87

2. When playing in the First Team, or being nominated as substitute for Football League Championship matches you will receive :-

    (a)   Bonus for the First 35 points of £100. per point.
               "   " 36 to 45 points of   £200. per point.
               "   " 46 to 55 points of   £300. per point.
               "   " 56 points and above of £400. per point.

For the purpose of assessing the Bonus payments contained in Clause 2a Points will be awarded on a basis of 2 points for a Win and 1 point for a Draw.

    (b)   In addition a sum of £50,000. will be distributed among the First Team Pool of players at the discretion of the Club Management if the Club wins the First Division Championship.

    (c)   £100. for a win and £50. for a Draw for Freindly Matches.

3. When playing or being nominated as substitute in Football Association or Football League Cup Ties, Home and Away

    (a)   A Match Bonus will be paid as follows:-

	Bonus.	Appearance Money.
Second Round	£300.	---
Third Round.	£300.	---
Fourth Round.	£400.	---
Fifth Round	£500.	---
Sixth Round.	£600.	---
Semi Final.	£750.	£500. each game.
Final.	£2000.	£1200. each game.

    (b)   In the event of any round in these competitions ending in a Draw half-bonus will be paid. Where a Round is played over two legs, a player playing in one game only will receive a full bonus payment.

    (c)   Talent money for winning the Football Association Cup, or gaining entry into the European Cup Winner Cup of £30,000. will be divided among the players taking part, at the discretion of the Club Management.

    (d)   If the Club gains entry into the UEFA Cup Competition by winning the Football League Cup Competition an amount of £30,000. will be distributed among the players taking part at the discretion of the Club Management.

4.   (a)   When playing, or being called on as a Substitute in the European Champions Cup Competition the following payments will be made :-

	Appearance Money Each Game.	Round Bonus.
First Round	£300.	£350.
Second Round	£350.	£500.
Third Round	£400.	£750.
Semi-Final.	£500.	£1500.
Final	£1200.	£3000.

My first big contract

Chapter 2

ACROSS THE WATER
Season 1981-82

Once I regained my fitness, season 1981-82 began in the unglamorous, training ground, early morning kick-offs of the Lancashire League Division One, where the Manchester United 'A' team plied their trade and I came into the side for the third fixture of the campaign. Many must have wondered what the gangling skinhead in the red shirt was going to produce and would have been pleasantly surprised that it was the 'A' team's season that I kick-started rather then half a dozen opposition defenders.

The opening two games had produced a 0-0 draw at Chorley and a 2-0 defeat at The Cliff against Wigan Athletic, so it had not been the best of starts, but that was soon to change with the introduction of the new centre forward. Lining up alongside the likes of Billy Garton, Graeme Hogg and Clayton Blackmore, Everton were soundly beaten 3-1, with the newcomer scoring twice.

My presence seemed to boost our confidence a little and we set off on an unbeaten run of seven games. Dropping down to 'B' team level did little to stem my enthusiasm and on November 14th I scored a hat-trick against Blackburn Rovers. Something of a parting gift, as this was my last United appearance until the end of January.

Returning to Old Trafford and available for selection again, I was rather surprisingly elevated to reserve team status, following an appearance with the Youth team against Leeds United in FA Youth Cup fourth round replay. At this time, we were doing well in this competition, having disposed of Walsall, against whom I scored one of our three goals, Liverpool and then Leeds.

Appearing at inside right against Nottingham Forest reserves at the City Ground, my performance was enough to ensure that I kept my place in the line-up for the following fixture at Sheffield Wednesday, where I contributed to our 4-1 victory.

"I had an important matter to attend to at Old Trafford. The signing of my first professional football contract"

My days in the lower regions of professional football, at 'A' and 'B' team level' were now a thing of the past as I quickly settled into the more competitive arena of the Central League, where experienced journeymen often lay in wait of unsuspecting youngsters.

I missed a couple of reserve fixtures following my two-goal performance at Sheffield, which were surprisingly lost, but upon my return, against Leeds on March 20th, we were only defeated three times in the remaining twelve fixtures. Ironically, I did not play in any of those defeats!

On March 8th, my dreams of playing in the Manchester United first team and also against Linfield, my boyhood foootballing first love, were shattered as I was under treatment for an ankle injury and fighting to be fit for an FA Youth Cup tie the following week.

Ron Atkinson had been suitably impressed with my performances in the Central League side to consider giving me my first senior outing and felt that making that big step up in my native city would have made my debut that little bit easier.

United's 1981-82 First Division campaign had stuttered along and their form had been inconsistent, to say the least. After failing to win any of their opening four fixtures, they went on an unbeaten run of eleven games. Three consecutive games at the end of March and the beginning of April, along with only five goals in eight fixtures between February 20th and April 7th emphasised the well debated point that the manager had a problem up front. It was also obvious to even the most blinkered of supporters that the League Championship was, for yet another year, not going to rest in the United boardroom. A place in Europe was, however, a distant possibility.

With little to lose, yet determined to grasp something from a somewhat uneventful season, Ron Atkinson threw caution to the wind and surprised many by introducing me to the first team squad for the trip to Brighton on April 24th. I was completely unaware that the manager had me in his plans and it wasn't until he called me into his office on the Friday morning that I knew anything about it.

Have you got a suit?" he asked me, as I sat with a blank expression on my face in reply. Assuming that I did possess such an item of attire, as I failed to give him much of a reply, he dispatched me to my lodgings to pack it with an overnight bag for the trip south. I was in a daze.

Thinking I was just going along for the ride, in order to gain a little match-day experience, it came as something of a shock when I was named as substitute.

Sitting on the bench, I watched United make hard work of a stubborn and competitive Brighton side. A thirty-yard drive from Bryan Robson almost gave United the lead in the 24th minute, but it struck the angle of the post and the bar and rebounded to safety. Ashley Grimes hit the side netting, as the home side were constantly pinned back in their own half. Frank Stapleton, a regular selection despite only having scored once in eighteen games, also came close after the interval, but it was one of those games that the onlookers had down for a 0-0 draw since the early stages.

With a UEFA Cup place high on his agenda, Ron Atkinson decided that he had little to lose by introducing a sixteen year old substitute into the fray for the remaining thirteen minutes of the game. After warming up, I was told to get stripped as I was going on in place of Mike Duxbury.

I was eager to get involved and being something of an unknown, the Brighton defence had little idea what to expect, but my introduction did little to create much in the way of interest as many began heading for the exits as the minutes began to tick away.

With only three minutes to go, Ray Wilkins hit a pass wide to the right, which found me unmarked. Without much thought, I continued the movement with a pass to Frank Stapleton, who in turn laid the ball back into the path of the on-running Wilkins. Ray was never a noted goalscorer, but the former Chelsea player hit the ball into the bottom corner of the net from around thirty yards out. This was enough to earn United the points and me a £600 win bonus. Not bad for thirteen minutes work and I should add that at that time, I was only earning £16 per week!

The win was also a vital two points for United in their quest for European football and unknown to me at the time was the start of illustrious, but unfulfilled career.

Ron Atkinson (Manchester United manager)
"I remember sitting down with the coaches at Old Trafford on Friday and telling them I was going to stick the kid Whiteside in at Brighton the following day. I just had a hunch. Right away you could see the lad was something special. They talk about his aggression. But the only way he ever hurt anyone was with his ability".

Two days after making my League debut, I returned to the normality of youth-team football as the United youngsters contested the 1st leg of the FA Youth Cup final against Watford at Old Trafford. To the surprise of both our supporters and ourselves, the Hertfordshire lads weathered the waves of early United attacks and recorded something of a shock 3-2 victory.

Taking the lead in the 33rd minute, Watford, with their goalkeeper Potts making a string of fine saves, kept United at bay until a minute before the interval when Mark Dempsey equalised. In the second half they once again proved their worth by storming into a 3-1 lead, before Clayton Blackmore pulled one back five minutes before time.

Following my League debut at Brighton, I found myself once again named as substitute as Southampton visited Old Trafford the following Saturday. Much to my disappointment though, there was no call to "get stripped" following a few jaunts up and down the touch line, as United plodded out another 1-0 victory.

The second leg of the Youth Cup Final, on May 6th, produced a match that would have graced any stage, as we pulled out all the stops, stretching the game into extra time.

> "Thinking I was just going along for the ride, in order to gain a little match day experience, it came as something of a shock when I was named as substitute"

A Billy Garton own goal in the 10th minute increased Watford's aggregate lead, but we refused to let it bother us too much and immediately set about searching for some consolation. Thanks to Mark Hughes, we reduced their advantage twenty minutes later, but within six minutes, the home side once again held a two goal advantage. After the interval, play was end to end and certainly provided the spectators with value for money. Mark Dempsey and Mark Hughes managed to prise open the home defence to make it 3-2 in our favour and put the tie level at 5-5. We had half an hour to win the coveted trophy.

An Andy Hill own goal as the additional thirty minutes got under way put Watford back in front, but minutes later, I managed to head an equaliser to keep our hopes alive. Mine and my team mates joy was short lived once again, as Watford scored what was to prove the winning goal three minutes later. Losing 7-6 on aggregate was certainly hard to take, as we felt that we had done enough to win the game.

Graham Taylor (Watford manager)
"Norman is going to be a fine player. The most vital asset of all for a forward is, knowing where the opposition goal is and what to do with the ball. He knows. If he continues his development without having any of these qualities taken from his play, then I'm sure he will be a United player for years."

Despite having played only a quarter of an hour first-team football and a handful of Central League games, Northern Ireland manager Billy Bingham caused something of a shock in the football world by including my name in Northern Ireland's squad of forty players for the forthcoming World Cup. Many felt, including myself, that I was only named in case there were any injuries to the others between now and the end of the season. On the other hand though, amongst his forty players, he had named nine part-time Irish League players, so I suppose I had an outside chance of making the final squad.

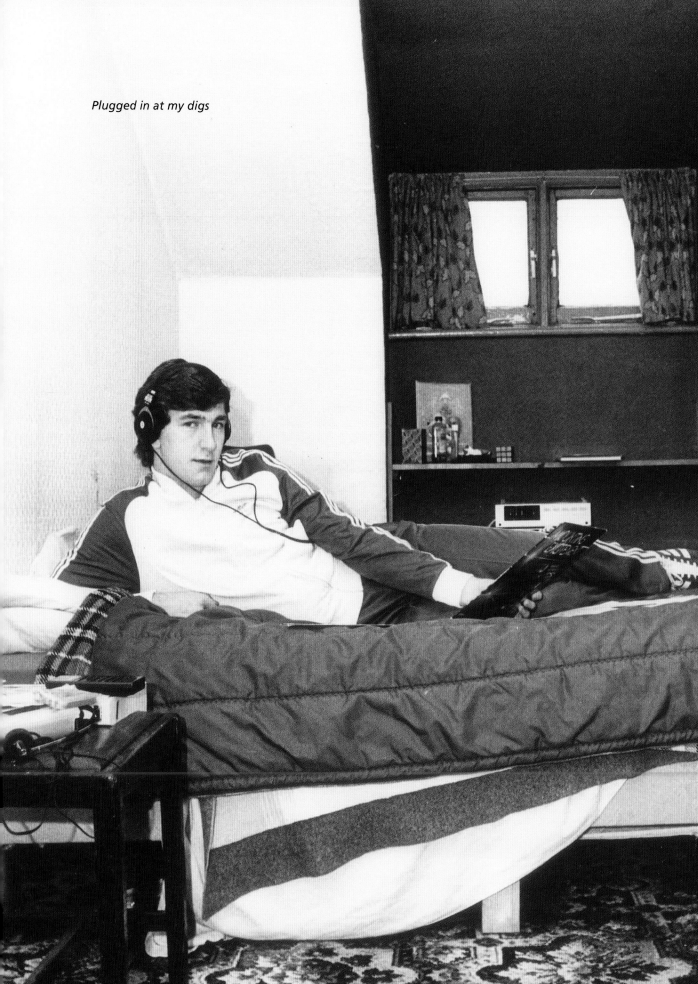

Plugged in at my digs

Ron Atkinson named me as substitute for the penultimate game of the season, but once again, to my disappointment, I failed to get off the bench at West Bromwich. This was, however, pushed to the side, as on the final Saturday of the 1981-82 season, when Stoke City visited Old Trafford, I was given my full first-team debut.

Our performance that afternoon showed a lot of what had been missing over the previous few weeks and we took the lead through Bryan Robson in the 42nd minute, with a close-range header at the back post. Stoke, still shaken by losing the opening goal, were dealt a second blow two minutes later, when Steve Coppell centred a perfect cross which I headed past Fox, for my first League goal. It was a moment to savour.

Following my full debut, United revealed that during the close season a special training schedule had been put together in order to help my development even further. I was to return to Belfast, where I would meet up with Olympic star Mary Peters, who would work on trying to improve my sprinting as it was perhaps an area that could improve my all-round play.

It turned out, however, to be an appointment that I was not to keep, as shortly afterwards I was a surprise (something of an understatement to be honest) inclusion in the narrowed down twenty-two man Northern Ireland World Cup squad for the forthcoming competition in Spain.

With the number of games that today's professionals have to play leading to much debate, I wonder what they would have made of United's decision to set off immediately after the final League game against Stoke for a three-match tournament in Canada, against Vancouver Whitecaps, Seattle Sounders and Hajduk Split? Especially with the World Cup only a matter of weeks away.

The tournament actually turned out to be a waste of time, with defeats against both the Vancouver and Seattle sides and I returned from my end-of-season jaunt for only a few days rest before re-packing my bags and heading for Spain. By a strange quirk of fate, I had to head to Brighton, where it had really all begun a few weeks earlier, to join up with my international team mates.

Before doing so, however, I had an important matter to attend to at Old Trafford. The signing of my first professional football contract.

*Showing no nerves
before the Group D
match with Austria*

Chapter 3

A SUMMER IN SPAIN
1982 World Cup Finals

The draw for the 1982 World Cup, the biggest tournament yet, did not offer Northern Ireland too much encouragement, pairing us in group five, with Honduras, Yugoslavia and the host nation Spain. England were slightly more fortunate, with France, Czechoslovakia and Kuwait as stable mates in group four, while Scotland on the other hand could wonder what they had done to deserve the likes of New Zealand, Brazil and the USSR.

Our base was Valencia and I was content to simply be in Spain as part of the Irish squad, because six months previously I was contemplating my future as I recovered from a cartilage operation. My only ambition then was half a dozen reserve games, to see if I could get sharp again.

Billy Bingham, who had played for Northern Ireland in the 1958 World Cup, was playing his cards so close to his chest that you would have thought that they were a pattern on his shirt, as he refused to commit himself either way regarding my selection when interviewed by the press. He simply said that he had been "impressed with my tremendous potential". Even I was kept in the dark as regards to his intentions.

They always say that you need a bit of luck at times and I certainly got a little of that prior to the opening fixture against Yugoslavia, as a training accident ruled Billy Hamilton out of the running for a place in the starting line-up. This also helped to ease the manager's selection headaches. Ironically, it was a kick on Billy's calf by my Manchester United team mate Jimmy Nicholl that caused the injury.

Even after the injury, Billy Bingham refused to reveal his team to the squad or the press, but he gave his clearest hint yet that I would find my name in the line up, when he told a press conference "You can speculate as much as you like. My team is clear in my mind and apart from a few little knocks, it is a nice blend of youth and experience."

"To reach the quarter finals in Spain was no mean feat and there was certainly no luck attached to it"

As the white-shirted Irish team walked out into the serene surroundings of the La Romereda Stadium, the name of Norman Whiteside was indeed amongst the chosen eleven, as part of the following team – Jennings, J Nicholl C Nicholl McClelland Donaghy, McCreery O'Neill McIlroy Armstrong, Hamilton and Whiteside. For me it was in some ways just another match, but it saw my name written into the World Cup record books as the youngest player ever to appear in the competition, at the age of 17 years and 41 days. This broke the record that was previously held by someone called Pele!

Under the sterling captaincy of Martin O'Neill we gave a thoroughly professional display, which at times frustrated the Yugoslavs, but it earned us a well-deserved point. Yugoslavia failed to show much in the way of imagination as they made only token attempts to break down our defence and for long periods, the game was played at a rather leisurely pace, with both teams settling for a draw well before the referee blew for full time.

Never having been overawed in any previous games, although I admit to having a few butterflies, I was determined to play as I normally did and my physical presence seemed to cause the more experienced opposition defence some concern. Perhaps at times my enthusiasm did get the better of me and it led to a second-half booking for a heavy tackle on Stojkovic, although it could also be classed as a form of revenge, as he had taken persistent liberties.

Billy Bingham (Northern Ireland manager)
"I thought of substituting him because the conditions were harsh and he had begun to flag. But he recovered well. Playing him was not a gamble. It wasn't even a calculated risk, because I knew he would match up to it."

I have to admit that at times I felt that being substituted would be a relief, as I was gasping for breath and my throat was so dry. I couldn't even call to my team mates as only a croak would have came out.

Back home in Danube Street Belfast, my mother and father, along with eleven-year-old brother Hugh had watched the game on television, shouting encouragement as if they were in the stand alongside the touchline instead of hundreds of miles away.

Comparisons to George Best had always been there, but following my international debut they seemed to increase ten- fold, but Billy Bingham, who had also managed George at this level was quick to jump into the debate, adding "there is no comparison between the two. They have absolutely nothing in common and I'm sure the lad would be very relieved if everybody just forgot all about George Best".

I simply echoed his sentiments, even though such comparisons were flattering, while also unfair, as George was a genius and I don't think there will ever be another player like him. Calling me the new George Best was ridiculous. It also puts a lot of pressure on me."

"In some ways it was just another match, but my name was written into the World Cup record books as the youngest player ever to appear in the competition, a record previously held by Pele!"

Aileen Whiteside (Norman's mother)
"My nerves were wrecked during the World Cup. I 'phoned him in Spain and he was as cool as anything. That's the kind of boy he is. Nothing flusters him. You wouldn't believe how confident and mature he is for a lad of seventeen."

Our inspired performance against Yugoslavia should have been enough to ensure that the footballing nobodies of Honduras, our next opponents, would be defeated and practically ensure our progress into the quarter-finals. As it was, we failed to reproduce that form and were possibly fortunate to draw 1-1. This result meant that nothing short of a win against Spain would be enough to progress in the competition.

The game against Honduras began favourably, with Gerry Armstrong giving us the lead as early as the 8th minute, as he followed in on a Sammy McIlroy free kick which hit the cross bar and was headed on by Chris Nicholl. Strangely though, they unsettled us more than the Yugoslavs and continually put our defence under pressure, which was to finally pay off with an equaliser in the 58th minute.

This time, however, I did not survive being substituted, although my performance was on par to that of my team mates and I was replaced by Noel Brotherston as the manager sought a breakthrough from a different angle, which was not to come.

While we now required a win, Spain only needed a point to go through. Ever confident, we set about the job in hand in the confines of the torrid atmosphere of the Luis Casanova Stadium in Valencia, but the match evolved into a rather cynical confrontation. Spain rarely caring or abiding within the rules of the game.

Some of the Spaniards tackles and tactics could easily have unruffled lesser sides, but we chose to ignore them the best we could. The decision to do so eventually paid off when Gerry Armstrong latched onto a loose ball in the 47th minute, following a cross from Hamilton, that the Spanish goalkeeper Arconada failed to hold,

The remainder of the game was played on a knife edge, as we fought to hold on to our lead. It all took a lot out of me, with the manager deciding to substitute me, bringing on Sammy Nelson, with twenty minutes to go. It was a substitution which was also rather inevitable following the sending off of Mal Donaghy ten minutes before.

Hold on to our lead we did, bringing emotional scenes at the end of the game as we had, against the odds, obtained a notable and memorable victory, progressing into the quarter finals. I believe that the scenes of celebration were equally as fervent back in Northern Ireland, with the pubs doing a roaring trade.

"While we now required a win, Spain only needed a point to go through"

Back in the our upmarket Side Solar Hotel after the match, I phoned home and was told that there were people dancing in the street outside my home and I think it was then that I realised what was actually happening to me. We all celebrated in an equally boisterous fashion, with the late-evening, early-morning air vibrating to the sound of 'When Irish Eyes Are Smiling' again and again.

Amongst the Irish contingent was an Englishman who pulled me aside and gratefully accepted a cold beer from me before saying "remember before you came to Spain that I wanted you back in Manchester as soon as possible to shape up your speed? Forget it."

Ron Atkinson (Manchester United manager)
"He's a big lad and still growing. I reckon he'll be tipping the scales at a good thirteen stones before he has finished developing. That is certainly going to put the wind up quite a few defenders in the future."

Moving into the second phase of the competition, we were paired with Austria and France and in our first quarter final match faced the first mentioned in the Vicente Calderon Stadium with the temperature touching ninety degrees.

Although desperately looking forward to the game, there was the nagging worry, shared by Sammy McIlroy and Billy Hamilton, of picking up a second yellow card which would have brought an enforced omission from the crucial second group D match against France. A game we would probably have had to win to make it into the semi-finals. Receiving a booking was a distinct possibility due to my sometimes-barnstorming style of play, which had been noted by players and referees alike. Billy Bingham was, however, unperturbed by such a possibility and had no special pre-match instructions for me.

My worn Northern Ireland World Cup '82 shirt

Having already defeated Spain, Austria did not cause us any worries and as the game progressed, we were beginning to enjoy the best of the early exchanges. Taking the game to the Austrians, who were clearly unsettled, we took the lead in the 25th minute, when Gerry Armstrong's precise cross was headed past Koncilia by Hamilton.

Jim Platt, playing in goal in place of the injured Pat Jennings, had little to do up until our goal, but after the interval when the Austrians made a couple of substitutions, the game took a completely different outlook. Five minutes after the restart, Pezzey scored the equaliser after Jimmy Nicholl's attempted clearance hit the post and rolled along the line.

Slowly they began to dominate the game and minutes after Brotherston had replaced me, they took the lead when Hintermaier scored. Thinking that they had secured the points, they began to ease up slightly, not realising that they were inviting trouble. Fifteen minutes from the end, they were punished for this discretion, when Hamilton headed home Jimmy Nicholl's cross. This was enough to earn us a point, but it was a game many felt that we should have won.

This left us with no alternative than to beat the French, who were a team well capable of winning the tournament itself, but it was a mountain that would prove difficult to climb. We required goals, not only to beat them but also to ensure that we had a better goal difference than the Austrians.

It was a case of all-or-nothing and we sometimes threw caution to the wind. This resulted on us being caught out on four occasions by the more experienced French, with Gerry Armstrong snatching a consolation strike from one of my passes, with the score already sitting at 3-0.

Despite the overall disappointment, the experience of the competition played a big part in my footballing education and I was now set upon winning a place in Manchester United's first team at the start of the following season. I didn't expect to be given a starting place automatically, I could wait, but the past few weeks had whetted my appetite for the big time and I certainly wanted more.

I must add that the competition not only gave me much experience as a player, but also made quite a difference to my bank account as each of the Irish players received £18,000 for our notable performances. A windfall for someone who was earning only a few pounds per week a short while before.

Returning to Britain following the defeat against France I received something of a hero's welcome from a large number of people who had gathered at Heathrow Airport to meet the team and I suspect that quite a few of those would not have recognised me at all some two months earlier.

Having only been familiar with the environments of Old Trafford and the Cliff training ground with Manchester United, I found the whole World Cup experience most enjoyable, especially the day-to-day involvement with the rest of the squad.

Sammy McIlroy and Jimmy Nicholl, I obviously knew from United, but the rest of the lads were something of a mixed bunch. There were the experienced professionals such as Pat Jennings with 91 caps, Martin O'Neill with 43 and Sammy and Jimmy with 56 and 43 respectively. At the other end of the scale, there was Bobby Campbell of Bradford, Jim Cleary of Glentoran and Felix Healy of Coleraine all with two caps apiece. Then there was Johnny Jamieson, George Dunlop and myself with none.

To be involved with the likes of Jennings, O'Neill and of course our manager Billy Bingham was great, as there was so much to learn. Big Pat, a tremendous goalkeeper, with hands like shovels, made the goalmouth seem so small and it was

On the ball against Austria
in our Group D clash on 1st July 1982

always a challenge to put the ball past him. It was also really strange finding myself in the same team as him, as Pat was winning his seventh cap for Northern Ireland on the day I was born!

If I had to single out one player who helped me the most during our time in Spain, then it would have to be my roommate Sammy McIlroy. Sammy was now a Stoke City player, having left Old Trafford in February, but was a great lad and still took me under his wing, as he knew something of what I was going through, having been thrust into the United side against Manchester City in November 1971 and scoring on his debut.

Sammy was our captain during the 1986 World Cup campaign and it is little surprise that he went on to a career in management. Hopefully he will achieve the success that he deserves.
Another of my team-mates of that time, our captain in Spain, who went on to a career in management and a successful one at that, was Martin O'Neill. There was never any doubt that Martin would make a success as a manager, even as a player, he showed great qualities in leadership and was an inspiration to everyone.

Having tasted domestic and European Cup success with Nottingham Forest, under the managership of Brian Clough, he used his experience wisely and encouraged everyone around him. Martin was someone I enjoyed playing alongside and cannot praise highly enough. It was certainly no surprise to me that he worked his way through the divisions to land one of the top jobs in the country with Celtic and to be linked with other top managerial vacancies when they become available. A top man.

"Despite the overall disappointment, the experience of the competition played a big part in my footballing education and I was now set upon winning a place in Manchester United's first team"

Our manager, Billy Bingham, was another winner and someone I also cannot praise highly enough, as he had the belief in me as an untried youngster. Many would never have considered such a young inexperienced player for a major World competition, but Billy knew that I would not let him down and I am always grateful to him for giving me the opportunity of playing on such a stage. One that not everyone has the pleasure of doing.

To reach the quarter finals in Spain was no mean feat and there was certainly no luck attached to it. Billy had limited resources, but made the most of what he had, blending together a team that played for each other and were not overawed by the big occasion. Perhaps we should have done more over a period of time, but that is no reflection on the manager's ability. He was a gentleman and a pleasure to know and play under and like Ron Atkinson, a manager to whom I shall always be grateful.

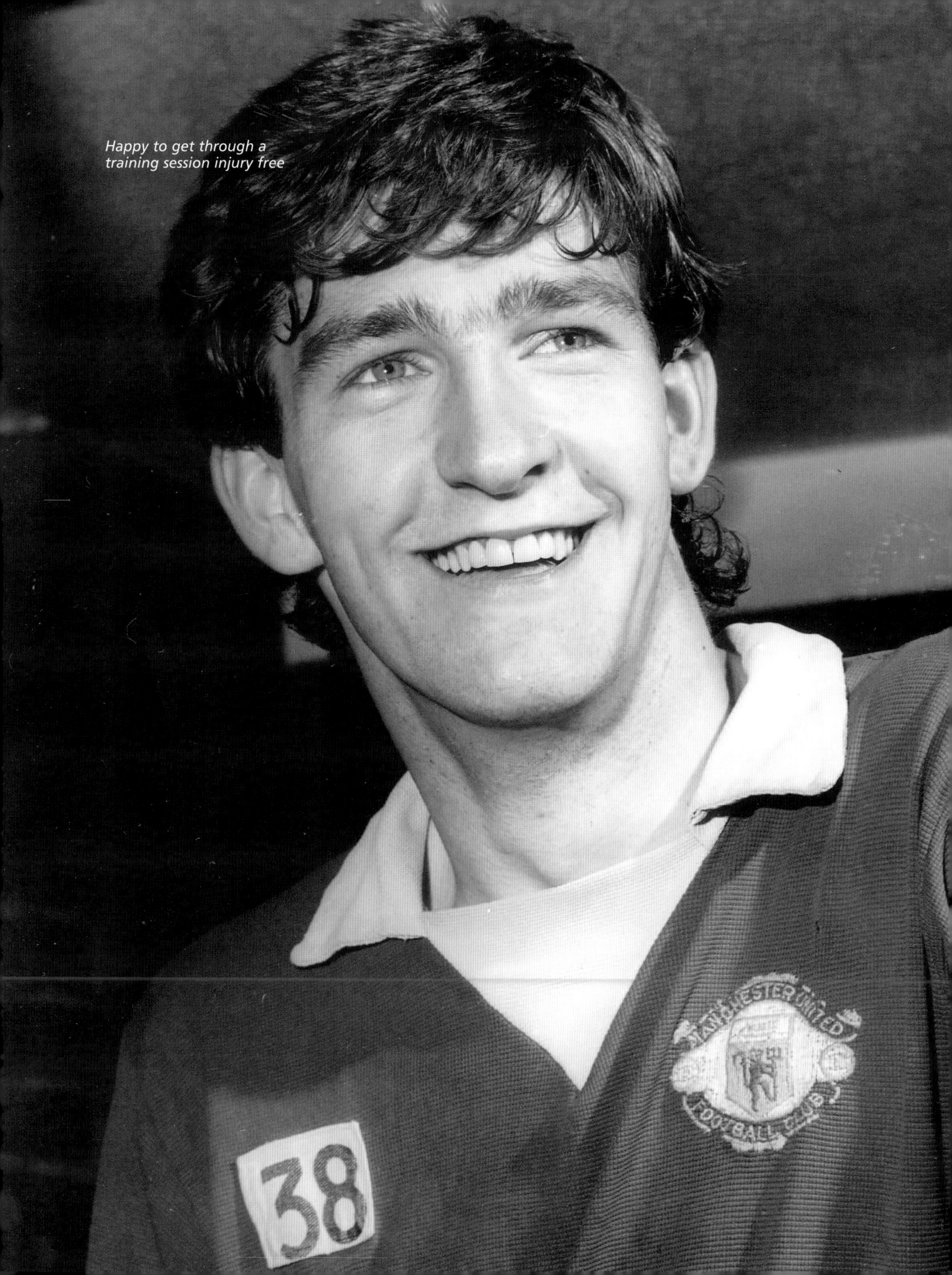

Happy to get through a training session injury free

Chapter 4

LIVING UP TO THE PROMISES
Season 1982-83

In a matter of weeks, I had gone from the somewhat obscurity of the Central League to the greatest footballing stage available for any professional – the World Cup Finals. I was no longer "Norman who?" but a household name throughout the country. Despite this sudden burst into the spotlight, the periods of relaxation, of what was left of the close season, began to bring moments of concern as the date for returning to training at The Cliff drew nearer. Although I had finished season 1981-82 in the Manchester United first team, I had spent some considerable time wondering where I stood in manager Ron Atkinson's plans for the coming campaign.

My fears were soon cast aside, as the boss had watched my World Cup outings from close quarters and announced that I did indeed feature in his immediate plans and would be involved in the pre-season tour games.

The news of the manager's plans came as a huge relief, with the speculation surrounding the departure of Gary Birtles, a £1.25 million signing from Nottingham Forest, whose career at Old Trafford had stuttered along, easing my worries even further.

It was not all roses, however, as it was soon to materialise that United had their eyes on Wolves striker Andy Gray, with the manager admitting his interest. Fortunately, for me at least, a £1million fee was put on the Wolves' player's head, placing him out of the reach of United.

The failure to capture Gray made me determined to claim a place in the United starting line up as the pre-season friendlies got under way. A place on the bench was all that was available for the first of those games at Aldershot, a match in aid of the South Atlantic Benefit fund. I was one of six second half substitutes and quickly adapted to the pace of the game and was unfortunate not to score with a chip which bounced of the cross bar.

> "I hadn't expected to be in the United side during the
> past season, even after the World Cup, so everything
> was really something of a bonus for me"

The Recreation Ground was quickly replaced with the more spartan surroundings of Icelandic club's Valur and AK Aureiri, where I attempted to outshine an old master, and one of my hero's. Now having to be content with 'guest appearances' around the globe, George Best faced his old club in the frozen north, but could do little to rekindle the fires of the past and warm the hearts of the Icelandic fans.

Against Valur, I grabbed two goals and was slightly embarrassed when the press suggested that I had shown numerous touches, which were once the hallmark of my Northern Ireland predecessor.

My best display in a United shirt to date came a few days later, in Dublin, playing in a testimonial match for former United player Don Givens. Although on the wrong side of the border, I felt near enough to home to be inspired into turning on something special, scoring two second-half goals in the 4-2 win.

One of those still remains in the old memory bank. I had my back to goal and with Jim Beglin breathing down my neck, a shrug of the shoulders took me clear of him and I followed up with a shot that beat the goalkeeper just inside the post.

Action from the Canon League Division One game away to Stoke City, 3rd September 1983

David Meek (The Manchester Evening News)

"He's raw and has a lot to learn, but has a natural talent. I've not seen anyone turn defenders so easily for a long time and I also saw him do it on the World Cup stage for Northern Ireland in Spain this summer. It is his ability in front of goal that I believe, will put him in the senior team."

George Best re-emerged in a Glentoran shirt, as we continued our pre-season preparations and he showed me what I had to aspire to, as he turned on a superb display in our native Belfast. I was rather disappointed with my own efforts upon my return home.

With the start of the build-up for the new season gathering pace, I began to feel the pressure of competing for a first- team place intensify, with Frank Stapleton, Gary Birtles, pre-season top scorer Scott McGarvey and myself, after the two forward positions.

I furthered my own cause for inclusion, when I returned to Zaragoza, the scene of my World Cup debut, to play in a four club tournament, with the headlines in the press proclaiming 'Norman Returns To Conquer'.

A 3-1 win over Hungarian side Honved, which saw me score one and make another, had the newspapers, in my opinion, going a bit over the top about my performance. In the Daily Mirror, Bob Russell wrote that I would be the reason that Ron Atkinson would not take an interest in Kevin Keegan any further!

Two goals against Bolton Wanderers at Old Trafford, in a testimonial match for former United physiotherapist Jim Headridge, on the eve of the new season, really put the ball in the manager's court. But a knock, which saw me replaced near the end left me in a sweat for a couple of days.

On the day before the big kick-off, all my worries had been for nothing, as I was named as Frank Stapleton's striking partner to face Birmingham City at Old Trafford. Whether or not I could command a regular place I was uncertain, but I had certainly been playing with much more confidence since the World Cup and would definitely make the most of my opportunity.

As Frank Stapleton's striking partner, I could not have wished for a better tutor and I came through that opening fixture with much credit. Although not getting on the score sheet, I made a telling contribution to United's 3-0 win, with involvement in the first goal, two minutes after the interval, heading on an Arnold Muhern corner for Kevin Moran to score.

"The old pros, usually look out for the young kids trying to make their mark in the First Division. They go out of their way to try and soften them up with a bit of physical stuff" said Frank Stapleton, the elder member of the United strike force and a player with much experience. "But after another dozen games, I'm certain a few of them will be able to testify that Norman Whiteside had been around".

Reflecting between myself and previous front line partner, Gary Birtles, Stapleton judged the latter as more of a runner, who enjoyed the freedom to move along the line, whereas he considered myself to be the type of player who you always liked to be in a certain area of the pitch.

Stapleton also revealed that prior to the World Cup Finals, the United coaching staff had wondered about letting me go to Spain. "I urged them to give him the go ahead and I believe we are going to see the benefit now."

Meeting George Best who turned out for Glentoran in the match at the Oval with Stephen Chick (the Glentoran mascot)

"The manager also said not so long ago that Norman could save the club a million in the transfer market. From what I have seen so far, I have no doubts that he is capable of doing exactly that."

I kept my place in the United side for the second fixture of the new season and looked forward to the game against Nottingham Forest with some relief as Gary Birtles had rejoined our opponents, making it one player less to compete against for a first team-place.

For the second consecutive fixture, we ran out 3-0 winners and I managed to open my scoring account for the season, netting the second in the 82nd minute. A sharp glancing header from a Bryan Robson cross after he had been released by Muhren.

A 3-1 reversal at West Bromwich followed, but I repaid Ron Atkinson's faith in selecting me by scoring three goals in the following two games, victories at both Everton and Ipswich.

"Although I was still only seventeen, I was quickly making a name for myself both on and off the pitch"

The Ipswich encounter, although a run-of-the-mill fixture, had an added incentive for me, as it brought me in direct opposition with Alan Brazil, who had been a transfer target of the manager's for some time. But by the end of the afternoon at a sun drenched Old Trafford, I had gained the upper hand over the Scot, with my two goals, the second of which was a half chip, half scoop over Cooper in the Ipswich goal.

"I do have a high regard for Brazil" the United manager said, "but I have plenty of praise for Norman's emergence this season. His potential is frightening. He's going to be a great player."

Against Ipswich, it took me only two minutes to open the scoring, latching onto a defensive mix up in their goal mouth. The Suffolk side managed to equalise and suddenly our sparkle was gone and it was not until the 73rd minute that we managed to regain the lead through Steve Coppell.

The result was put beyond any doubt four minutes from the end, when I managed to chip Paul Cooper in the Ipswich goal from the edge of the penalty area. It was a goal worthy of winning any match even though I say so myself.

George Best
"The more I see him, the more I am impressed."

There were numerous articles now appearing in the national press following my performances in United's opening fixtures and I was, rather embarrassingly named the new idol of the Stretford End. I was in fact no more than an average teenager and even then that was something of an understatement.

"I was constantly asked about my comparison to George Best, but there was no comparison, except that we both happened to come from Belfast and were discovered by the same scout and signed for Manchester United. I had never even seen George Best play before coming up against him in the pre-season friendlies.

My ambitions in those early days were nothing high flying. I couldn't even drive at the time, but began taking lessons and decided to replace the No. 94 Corporation bus to the ground with a Ford Escort. My 'image' had also taken a change, as I began to let my hair grow a little to escape the 'skinhead look' that I had.

In my spare time, I was little different from any other teenager and enjoyed going to the cinema, playing snooker and the odd disco. As I began to earn more money, I began to spend a bit more on clothes, mainly casual stuff, as a dark blue pin stripe suit was good enough for match days. A bit more modest a wardrobe compared to today's Old Trafford stars. Life in Manchester certainly suited me, but it did cause my mother some concern as she felt that I was too young to be away from home. She did, however, always emphasise that she would never stand in my way despite the doubts in the back of her mind.

She was also always reminding me that there were so many things that could go wrong and that numerous others had had their heads turned by all the attention and the money. The latter, she advised me to be sensible with and to put some away for the future as well as making sure that I had enough to buy myself the kind of things that a mother would normally buy for her son, like underwear and toiletries.

"Watch out for the girls" was another of her warnings, but it was drink that she really went to town about. "One drink leads to another and you know what two drinks lead to?" was one of her favourite sayings.

My first taste of European Club football came against Valencia at Old Trafford in a UEFA Cup tie on September 15th, a disappointing goal less draw, which saw me take the brunt of the Spaniards tackling. I felt that Miguel Tendillo singled me out for some 'special attention', kicking me all over the park. Although I left the field covered in bruises, I received little in the way of protection from the Czechoslovakian referee.

"Sometimes, I found it hard to believe that things have gone so well and so quickly"

Early bookings for the visitors should have led to subsequent sendings off as the game progressed, but the weak hearted official neglected his duties. Although he did find the time to book yours truly after I got involved with Carreto. Looking back, it was all part of my learning process.

The return leg in the Louis Casanova stadium failed to rekindle the memories of my first visit to the arena a few months previously with Northern Ireland, when we defeated the hosts in that never to be forgotten World Cup win. For a while, it looked as if United were about to do a repeat, as we lead from a Bryan Robson goal at half time.
Valencia equalised with a debatable penalty, when Rises fell over Kevin Moran's outstretched leg inside the box, snatching a second through Roberto, when our defence failed to clear a free-kick.

In all honesty, we should have won, as Remi Moses and myself both spurned scoring chances and I felt that the referee once again favoured the Spaniards, as tension ran high both on and off the pitch. Many though, felt that I was very fortunate indeed not to be sent off after a foul on Botubot. My 'victim' himself was later booked for taking out some revenge on his assailant.

Having seen off the challenge of Gary Birtles, I suddenly found myself faced with another, with the arrival of Peter Beardsley from Vancouver Whitecaps. The newcomer took over from me against Bournemouth in the Football League Cup. Once again, I managed to come out on top, replacing him as substitute and then playing in the second leg, with that solitary outing being Beardsley's only appearance in a United shirt.

Regaining my place following my 'rest', I made the only goal of the game for Bryan Robson against Stoke City on October 9th, as United moved into top position in the First Division, but picked up an ankle injury which was to keep me out of the Northern Ireland squad to face Austria in a European Championship match in Vienna. Billy Bingham, my Northern Ireland team manager called my absence a "major headache", but I did not see my position in the side as being so important. However, I might have made some telling contribution in our 2-0 defeat.

In November, as my ankle injury eased off, I was voted 'Newcomer of the year' by the Sports Writer's Association and as well as returning to the United side, I reclaimed my place in the Northern Ireland side to face World Champions West Germany in Belfast. Somewhat against the odds, we managed to cause the vastly experienced German defence numerous problems and recorded a momentous and memorable 1-0 victory.

Back with United, we maintained our challenge at the top of the First Division, attempting to bring the title to Old Trafford for the first time since 1967, whilst also enjoying the additional involvement in the Football League Cup, which was going under the guise of the Milk Cup. Having played in the third round tie against Bradford City, which ended in a 0-0 draw, I found myself omitted from the team that travelled to Yorkshire for the replay, although I did manage to make an appearance as substitute for Steve Coppell. I remember the Daily Mirror headline stating that 'Norman Takes A Rest Cure', but I think that they were simply using a polite way of saying that I had been dropped, as both myself and the team as a whole had not been playing well, taking only ten points from the previous nine League fixtures.

Having gone a run of some fifteen games without a goal between mid-September and the end of November, I suppose I didn't really deserve to be in the starting line-up. However, the manager never had any hesitation in naming me in the side, although he must have had a few occasions when he deliberated over my selection.

Despite United winning the Bradford replay 4-1, without much in the way of assistance from me, I found myself back in the starting line-up to face Norwich City at Old Trafford. I also received reassurance from assistant manager Mick Brown that the form which had thrust me into the lime light would soon return and that I was still something of an apprentice amongst tradesmen. It was still something of a worry though, as scoring goals was always something that had come naturally to me.

Norwich were beaten 3-0, Bryan Robson grabbing a double and Arnold Muhren the other and with a Milk Cup tie against Southampton following four days later I thought that I would once again be omitted from the starting line up. Surprisingly though, Ron Atkinson kept the same eleven and I repaid his faith in me with our second goal, two minutes from the end, in the 2-0 win. I am certain that many of the departing crowd heard my sigh of relief as the ball hit the back of the net.

Three days later, I was back amongst the headlines as I followed up my Milk Cup strike with the only goal of the game against Watford at Vicarage Road. 'Norman Swoops To Conquer' and 'A Bumper Bundle From Whiteside' were just two of the many in the following two days sports pages.

The spring was back in my step and the doubts that I had shared with everyone one else were banished, as another 'above average' performance followed against Notts County, scoring once again in a 4-0 win. What had been more of a worry

at this time was in fact my driving test, but I managed to pass it at my first attempt, although my team mates tried to imply that the only reason that I did in fact pass was because of my name and not my driving ability.

Unfortunately, I couldn't make it three League games in succession with a goal and following the 0-0 draw against Swansea City, I found myself back alongside players of my own age, with selection for the United FA Youth Cup side against Derby County in the 3rd round of the competition. Because of my senior experience, I was perhaps a bit more closely marked than normal and failed to make much of an impression in a rather scrappy game that saw Derby leave Old Trafford with a draw.

As 1982 came to an end, United stuttered along with only one win in four League games and I found myself missing the 3-0 defeat at Coventry. I also managed to continue to steer clear of any criticism that was directed towards the strikers for the lack of goals being scored. I think that still being something of a novice in the senior game helped divert the criticism in the opposite direction. Obviously, the coaching staff pushed me when necessary and they also spent a lot of time working on the areas of my game that they felt needed developed.

"Frank Stapleton came across as a rather quiet individual, keeping himself to himself, but I found him a big help..."

Criticism, however, did come my way, not from anyone at United though, but from the press.

Following our 2-0 FA Cup 3rd round victory over West Ham United, the team and perhaps more so me came in for a fair bit of criticism, but we were only too aware that our performances were not up to scatch.

Patrick Barclay (The Guardian)
"Whiteside is an admirable young player, but he is beginning to look more and more like a seventeen year old as his touch deserts him and should be replaced by Macari."

It was obvious, even to me, that I would be unable to perform in a similar fashion to that which had seen me break into the United and Northern Ireland sides and also maintain a high standard of play throughout the current season. Whether it was that particular article in the Guardian, or that I had simply worked myself out of the lean spell that I had been going through, I do not know, but I suddenly found myself turning in the sort of performances that the management, supporters and of the course, the press, expected of me.

Against Birmingham City at St Andrews, a game that United won 2-1, I opened the scoring just after the interval, while the following mid-week, although failing to score, I played my part in our 4-0 Milk Cup quarter-final tie against Nottingham Forest. We then played Forest, again at Old Trafford, three days later, winning only 2-0 this time, but I had by now redeemed myself in the eyes of many. Even some of the press returned to their complimentary headlines, with the Sunday Express exclaiming 'Kid Norman Supplies the Double Punch'.

James Mossop (The Daily Express)
"He is seventeen, gifted and strong. An Ulster boy with a touch of inventiveness and, in his case, a match winner whose name, Norman Whiteside, never reached the score sheet. But it was his cute and instant control that brought victory for United in the First Division's race to decide who comes second to Liverpool. Panic was etched on Forest's defensive faces

*In heaven with my Man Utd team-mates after our
FA Cup Final replay victory over Brighton & Hove Albion*

midway through the second half, when a sudden burst of skill took Whiteside through the scything tackles of desperadoes who helped to restore Forest's pride after their 4-0 mid-week defeat on the same pitch. They finally robbed the young sorcerer as he went to play his winning trick, but when he came at them a moment later the magic worked. With a dip of his shoulders and a nudge to one side, he sped past Willie Young and entered the penalty area on his way to goal. Full back Stuart Gray was foxed by the feints and dummies and a wild lunge sent Norman crashing. Coppell scored with the resulting penalty kick and United were on their way to victory."

Patrick Barclay (The Guardian)
"For sixty four minutes, Whiteside, the ugly duckling of the United team that, with move after move floundering on his lack of experience, looked just one player short of excellence. Yet ambition kept the young Ulsterman going and suddenly he turned into a swan, flying free in the penalty area, past Young and Gray, whose attempt at a tackle brought United their breakthrough from the penalty spot."

The spectre of Alan Brazil continued to haunt me, with constant newspaper headlines linking him with a move to Old Trafford and Ron Atkinson freely admitting his admiration for the player. He also stated that he was prepared to give me the rest of the season to prove that I was indeed worthy of my place in the side on a permanent basis and that he would take stock during the close season.

Face to face with Alan Brazil at Portman Road, Ipswich Town more-or-less ended what outside hopes we had of winning the title, holding us to a 1-1 draw. It was certainly disappointing, as it was yet another year without the name of Manchester United being inscribed on the trophy. Thankfully, we still had the FA Cup and the Milk Cup to play for. Not as important as 'the big one', but silverware never the less.

My first-team commitments had prevented me from playing against the Queen's Park Rangers youth team in a 0-0 draw at Loftus Road, but with the Old Trafford replay scheduled for mid-week I was able to step down a few rungs of the football ladder and turn out along with the lads that I had begun my career with. My experience had some sort of effect on the outcome of the game, which United won comfortably 4-0, as I scored twice and made one of the others.

Cup-ties were now the order of the day, coming thick and fast, as we pursued the two domestic trophies, with a trip to Highbury in the 1st leg of the Milk Cup semi-final first on the agenda. Pre-match press coverage brought to my attention that it had been some fifteen years since United had last won at the north London venue and that it had been the Gunners who wrecked United's last dream of cup glory in 1979. Both statistics gave me an added incentive to do well.

Right from the first blast of the referee's whistle we pushed forward, tormenting the Arsenal defence at every opportunity, with myself and strike partner Frank Stapleton, himself a former Arsenal player, in the thick of things.

With fourteen minutes gone, Remi Moses won the ball from Graham Rix, with a forceful tackle and found me unmarked on the edge of the Arsenal penalty area with an exquisitely floated pass. Meeting the ball on the half volley, I held my breath as it soared past the wrong-footed Pat Jennings to stretch the netting behind him.

It became increasingly difficult for Arsenal to mount any sort of threat on our goal, as we kept them pinned back in their own half. Three minutes before the interval, they suddenly found themselves 2-0 behind. This time I was the provider and not the scorer. Bryan Robson caught Talbot in possession and his pass found me in space, as I evaded my marker. My cross to the far post was ideal for Frank Stapleton, who took great delight in heading past Jennings As the game passed the

*Celebrating my goal with Mike Duxbury during
the Milk Cup Final against Liverpool 26th March 1983*

hour mark, our thoughts began to drift, perhaps rather prematurely, to Wembley, when Frank made it 3-0. But the twin towers became even more clearer when Steve Coppell scored our fourth six minutes later. Yours truly again setting up the chance, leaving Steve with little more to do than pick his spot.

Arsenal, to their credit, kept their heads up, as we relaxed a little with the game moving into the closing stages and they managed to score twice to give them a little bit of hope in salvaging some thing from the second leg at Old Trafford.

My partnership with Frank Stapleton was now slowly beginning to gel and perhaps now was the right time of the season for this to happen, with our involvement in both of the domestic cup competitions.

Much is written today about the help that Eric Cantona was in the development of the likes of David Beckham, Ryan Giggs, Paul Scholes, Nicky Butt and the Neville brothers, well Frank was similar to Eric in the way that he helped me. I not saying that he was as good a player as Eric, it is just that as a more experienced professional, he took the time to help in my development.

Frank was my mentor. I was already at United when he arrived, but he was a highly experienced forward both at club and international level, while I was still learning. Often in training, he would mention little things that he felt could help me, while if he spotted something during a game that he thought I had done wrong or could have done better or differently, then he would go over the incident, or whatever, in an effort to help me improve. This wasn't something that he was asked to do, but something that he did off his own back.

Frank came across as a rather quiet individual, keeping himself to himself, but I found him a big help and he played a major part in my early development as a player. I think that it is important that the more experienced players at a club should do their bit in helping the youngsters in the way that Frank and Eric did.

Frank Stapleton
"Norman and I have managed to get a good understanding of each others play. It has strengthened in the short time we have been together. Norman is not only a very good footballer, but also a big strong lad who won't allow the opposition to subdue him. A lot of experienced central defenders have got the message – Norman may be young, but he may not be intimidated and put off his game. We'll make mistakes at times like any other striking pair, but our partnership is improving all the time. It can only get better."

Another team mate, Ray Wilkins, in a newspaper interview after the Arsenal match, went as far as to suggest that it had been my best performance to date for United. A statement I wouldn't have argued with. For the time being!

From the Milk Cup to the FA Cup and before Arsenal could travel to Old Trafford seeking revenge, we had to give our thoughts over to latter competition and a 4th round tie against Derby County at the unimpressive Baseball Ground.

The surroundings mattered little to me and by the end of the afternoon, Ray Wilkins had to reassess his declaration of a few days earlier, as I turned in yet another favourable performance. I also scored the only goal of the game to take us through into the next round and prompt another flurry of newspaper headlines over the next couple of days.
'Norman's Day', 'Whiteside's Winner' and 'Norman the Conqueror' were only three of the many.

Bob Russell (The Daily Mirror)
"The way Norman is built, he is never going to be the quickest player in the world, but he more than compensates for that. He possesses tremendous strength, rare vision, outstanding courage, exceptional close control and a competitiveness and professional maturity that makes nonsense of his seventeen years".

Forming a defensive wall with Remi Moses in the 1983 Milk Cup Final

Second Division Derby County and their goalkeeper Cherry in particular, had defied us for most of the match and it was not until six minutes from time that the tie was settled. One of the countless Derby attacks was thwarted by Kevin Moran, who pushed the ball forward to Steve Coppell. Steve, an excellent crosser of the ball picked me out easily and I had little difficulty in beating the Derby 'keeper for my tenth goal of the season. We were into the quarter finals. My dip in form and that of the team as a whole was now firmly in the past.

Big games didn't really phase me that much and I tried not to think too much about the opposition, but I was about to find out how tough it really was at the top over the next few weeks, as our fixture list showed Arsenal in the Milk Cup semi-final second leg, Everton in the FA Cup sixth round and League fixtures against Liverpool and Manchester City.

The Milk Cup tie was never going to live up to the drama and excitement of the Highbury fixture, but a broken ankle suffered by Bryan Robson put added pressure on us all, forcing me back into more of a midfield role. As I had done quite a bit to dent Arsenal's cup ambitions in the 1st leg, I was marked a bit more closely this time around. I did, however, manage to shrug off their shackles for a couple of minutes, setting up Steve Coppell for one of the two goals that took United to Wembley for the first time in four years. By a strange quirk of fate, our next opponents were our Milk Cup Final opponents, Liverpool, so there was slightly more than a couple of points at stake. In front of a packed Old Trafford, we shared the spoils in a 1-1 draw. City were beaten, as were Everton in the quarter finals of the FA Cup, setting up a second semi-final meeting with Arsenal and the opportunity of a second Wembley Cup Final appearance.

Personal honours were also pushed my way, as I was voted the 'Robinson's Barley Young Player of the Month' for February as well as being nominated for the Professional Footballer's Player o the Year. Heady times, but my life style was not one of flamboyancy and I had little inclination to enjoy the high life.

"Criticism, however, did come my way, not from anyone at United though, but from the press"

I suppose it could all have been a bit bewildering, even though I had played for Northern Ireland in the World Cup, but at that time I only hoped to win and keep a regular place in the United first team. Now, I was in with a chance of playing in two Wembley Cup Finals.

Sometimes, I found it hard to believe that things had gone so well and so quickly. I felt that I had learned an awful lot during this season, especially from playing alongside somebody as good as Frank Stapleton.

I also kept in regular touch with my family in Belfast, but too many things seemed to be happening to be homesick at any time. Anyway, my life was now in Manchester as there was nothing left for me back in Ireland.

March 26th saw United at Wembley for the Milk Cup Final against our Lancashire rivals Liverpool. With captain Bryan Robson failing a late fitness test, we were going to find it tough, but we certainly had the potential to take the trophy back to Old Trafford for the first time.

I didn't find my first game under the twin towers too nerve-racking and enjoyed the wide-open spaces that the Wembley pitch provided, as we took the game to Liverpool in the opening stages. Our approach took Liverpool somewhat unawares, so much so that we managed to take the lead after only twelve minutes.

My 1983 Milk Cup Runners-up medal and Souvenir Programme

Milk Cup Final

OFFICIAL SOUVENIR PROGRAMME 70p

The Milk Cup

Liverpool
v
Manchester United

Saturday 26th March 1983 Kick~Off 3·00pm

Wembley Stadium

A long down field clearance from Gordon McQueen, after he had broken up a Liverpool attack, bounced in my direction. Controlling the ball on my chest, I brought it down and turned past Alan Hansen in almost one movement, before firing it past Bruce Grobbelaar. The strike, as well as giving United the lead, also gave me the honour of being the youngest player ever to score in a Wembley Cup Final.

As the game wore on, it began to look as if that goal was also going to be enough to earn me a winner's medal, despite the fact that some of our fire had been doused through injury to Arthur Albiston and Kevin Moran. But, with fifteen minutes remaining, Alan Kennedy struck an equaliser to dent our hopes.

A further injury to Gordon McQueen, saw him pushed onto the right wing and Frank Stapleton take up a somewhat alien position in central defence. Our hobbling defender almost immediately became the focal point of the whole game, as he pursued a loose ball towards the Liverpool penalty area, as full-time loomed close, only to find himself crudely upended by Grobbelaar.

If I had committed such a tackle then I am certain that I would have had the dressing room showers to myself, but to the amazement of almost everyone in the ground, even the Liverpool supporters, referee George Courtney only administered a booking. The course of the game was about to change.

Nine minutes into extra time, Ronnie Whelan hit a long-range shot over the head of Gary Bailey for what was to prove the winning goal. We were gutted and I admit that there were a few tears shed in the dressing room at the end as I felt physically and emotionally drained. This defeat though, was to act as the spur that would propel us back to Wembley for the final of the F. A. Cup a matter of weeks later.

I had, however, to pick myself up immediately, as Northern Ireland had a European Championship match, against Turkey in Belfast, four days later. Thankfully Billy Bingham gave me a couple of days off to rest, as he was fully aware what effect playing at Wembley could have on players. This certainly paid off, as I had a reasonably good game in our 2-1 win, which was played on a rain sodden pitch, making the going hard.

Although I was still only seventeen, I was quickly making a name for myself both on and off the pitch. I was now enjoying a good rapport with the United supporters, who appreciated my youthful enthusiasm and never-say –die attitude. The opposition support, on the other hand, I think saw me simply as a roughhouse type of player who was happy to kick anything and anybody that came my way. Some opponents thought little different, while others readily admitted that their initial impression was a little off the mark.

John Wile (West Bromwich Albion)
"I thought a few defenders would sort him out, but when we played United I realised I'd got him wrong. He was hit hard once or twice, but kept going and I remember even in the last few minutes, he caught me late after I had got in a header, just to remind me that he was still around. I was most impressed with his temperament, because he dished it out and took it back and there was no squealing. Norman's skills tend to be over looked. Certainly, I underrated them. He's so ungainly that he sometimes seems as if he's lost control, then he'll pull out a trick and be off. The lack of pace may always be there but, then again, if you can't get away from someone it's a good idea to knock them off balance which he can do."

Saturday April 16th saw the Red Army travel en-masse to Villa Park Birmingham, where our semi-final part two against Arsenal was to be played. The warm spring afternoon produced a memorable ninety minutes, fitting for the occasion, with the name of Norman Whiteside snatching the following day's newspaper headlines.

My 1983 Milk Cup Final Shirt

Arsenal took the lead ten minutes before the interval, from what was virtually their first attack of the afternoon. They had mounted sporadic flourishes into the United half, but with little success, so they were quite happy to turn around with a one goal advantage, confident of maintaining their lead throughout the second period. Their plans, and hopes, were in complete disarray four minutes after the re-start, as United pulled level through Bryan Robson.

Ashley Grimes, a replacement for the injured Arnold Muhren, played an inviting pass into the Arsenal penalty area. Uncharacteristically, the Gunners defence had given Robbo a little too much space and paid for their error when he turned past Talbot, before hooking the ball past Arsenal 'keeper Wood. It was fitting revenge, as Talbot had previously fouled him with three rash tackles, which had earned a booking.

At level pegging, the tie was anybody's, but in the 69th minute came the decisive strike.

Grimes, once again moved forward with the ball before splitting the Arsenal defence with a sublime pass in from the left. Moving in on it, I allowed it to bounce before volleying it past Wood's outstretched left hand and into the net. I knew I was going to hit either the target or the scoreboard as soon as I connected with the ball and I was fortunate that it was the latter.

'Whiteside's Ticket to Wembley', 'White Hot Norman's Wembley Warning' and 'Walk On The Whiteside' screamed out at me from the sports pages over the next couple of days.

David O'Leary (Arsenal)

"Somehow, I have never thought of him as a seventeen year old. From the day he arrived in the game, he has seemed to me to be about twenty-seven. I've been amazed at the ability of someone so young. He has marvellous control for a player of his youth and more important, of his size. There are few players capable of holding and screening the ball better. Normally youngsters in their first season find it very hard because the elder, harder men in the game set out to intimidate them. But Norman just can't be scared off. He showed right from the start that he can ride the heavy tackle and that there is no point trying it on him. Part of my job as a defender is to get out and win the ball. That isn't easy against Norman. We know that he isn't quick, but that doesn't make him any easier to play against. He can also turn you. Not as quickly as Kenny Dalglish does, but get too close and he will use his strength to get around. If that happens on the edge of the penalty area it can be disastrous because the lad knocks the ball away so well."

Part of our Wembley build up was spent in Majorca and Magaluf and it was in the Spanish sunshine that I celebrated my eighteenth birthday. Sitting under a large sombrero, it was difficult to believe that I was now only old enough to drink something stronger than the chilled coca-cola I enjoyed as the sun beat down, as my life had careered along like a juggernaut out of control for most of the past five years. I suppose, when I thought about it, I had the world at my feet, but the spectre of George Best was never far away and as I celebrated being an eighteen year old, my Northern Ireland compatriot was facing the indignity of a bankruptcy court and also admitting to being an alcoholic. The warning signs were certainly there for me to heed.

Failure to capture the First Division championship was always a millstone around our necks, as it had been so long since the name of Manchester United had been engraved on the famous old trophy. Occasionally, as in 1977, there had been compensation in an FA Cup win, so to our supporters, the forthcoming Wembley date against Brighton and Hove Albion was a very big occasion. It was obviously something special for the players as well, giving them the opportunity to taste success at Wembley so soon after the disappointment o losing out to Liverpool in the Milk Cup Final of a few weeks previously.

Arsenal's David O'Leary looks on as I smash home the winning goal in the FA Cup Semi-final

While the manager's final line-up was open to debate, with the likes of Ashley Grimes, Lou Macari and Laurie Cunningham all vying for a place, I was secretively confident that my name was already pencilled in to the starting line up.

The build up to the big day went well and on paper we should have won the trophy without too much of a problem. Wembley Cup Final's, however, as United had found to their cost in years gone by, don't always go as expected.

On a rain-soaked pitch, Brighton took the initiative in the thirteenth minute when Gordon Smith scored, following what was their first real attack.

Having played there before, I was certainly not overawed by the occasion and began to get a bit more involved as the game went on. Many of those packed on the vast terraces actually thought that I had scored the equaliser two minutes after the interval, but I had used my hand to help the ball past Moseley in the Brighton goal. A considerable number of those who thought that I had scored, were not long afterwards baying for my blood following a challenge on Ramsey, that they considered just a little too hard.

"Three days later, I was back amongst the headlines as I followed up my Milk Cup strike with the only goal of the game against Watford at Vicarge Road"

In the fifty-fifth minute, I was involved in our equaliser, when my glancing header across the face of the Seagulls goal, at the far post by Frank Stapleton. After that, we began to take control and when Ray Wilkins scored in the seventy-second minute, that should have been the game up sewn up. While our supporters filled the north London air with songs of triumph, Brighton, although a little down, had other ideas.

With only four minutes remaining, they forced a late corner. Grealish, hitting the low corner from Case first time found Stevens around ten yards out and with the United defence caught flatfooted, he slipped the ball past Gary Bailey to level the scoring.

Extra time was now a formality, although it was something that we certainly did not want as the heavy pitch had taken quite a bit out of us. Most were simply content to see the additional thirty minutes out and come back the following week for a replay, allowing us time to recompose ourselves and return refreshed.

Such an opportunity, however, almost never materialised, as with only thirty seconds remaining, Case once again prised open our defence, threading the ball through to Robinson, who quickly outpaced Kevin Moran. Turning inside Gordon McQueen, he spotted Smith unmarked to his right.

Squaring the ball to his team-mate, who was only about ten yards out, the activity in the goal mouth seemed to become one of those slow-motion replays that you see, with the Brighton player looking more than certain to score. Thankfully, but to what must have been Gordon Smith's eternal horror, he allowed himself one touch too many and Gary Bailey managed to block the ball. Brighton's moment of glory was gone.

If I was completely honest, I didn't play up to my usual standards. I was also disappointed in some of the after match criticism that came my way regarding the challenge on Ramsey. It was hard, but no different from hundreds of others that I had made over the years. It was unfortunately a tackle that kept the Brighton player out of the replay.

HOVE ALBION
BRIGHTON

REPLAY

ASSOCIATION CHALLENGE CUP FINAL

FOOTBALL ASSOCIATION CHALLENGE CUP COMPETITION

BRIGHTON & HOVE ALBION

CUP FINAL

Saturday 21st May 1983 Kick-Off 3.00pm

MANCHESTER UNITED

Wembley Stadium

Official Souvenir Programme 80p

My FA Cup Winners Medal along with both the original and replay programmes

Chris Ramsey (Brighton and Hove Albion)
"If it had been me, I would have been sent off. These things happen in football and I'm not having a go at Norman. He's a brilliant player, but he did me and he should not have got away with it. In a League game he would have been booked. Norman is a better footballer than me. That's why I'm a full back. I've no hard feelings, but he is already a great player and I didn't think that the challenge was necessary."

I obviously received a 'warm' reception from the Brighton supporters as we took the field for the replay, but they were simply ignored as I was firmly focused on the game, as were the rest of the lads and there was no way that we were going to throw away our second chance.

It took us only twenty-four minutes to open the scoring and by half-time, we were three in front with the match all but won.

After an exchange of passes between Arthur Albiston and myself, I found Alan Davies, who in turn passed inside to Bryan Robson, whose first-time shot ended up in the left-hand corner of the Brighton goal to give us the lead. Four minutes later, as Gordon McQueen caused confusion in the Brighton penalty area following Arnold Muhren's corner, I headed the ball past Moseley to make it two. This goal saw the record books having to be re-written, as I became the youngest player to score in a FA Cup Final and also the first to score in two Wembley Finals in the same season.

Two minutes before the interval Bryan Robson made it three, heading home Muhren's free kick.

The second half was simply a formality, with Arnold Muhren receiving his reward for an outstanding contribution to the match, scoring our fourth from the penalty spot after Stevens pulled down the rampaging Robson. I should actually have made it five, but Moseley managed to get his fingers to the ball, pushing it onto the bar.

Some people said that I tended to turn it on for the big games and that has always been a habit of mine. I would really like to be hitting the target more consistently in the League, although there is no harm in scoring in Cup Finals. I felt that I really ought to be scoring every other game.

I hadn't expected to be in the United side during the past season, even after the World Cup, so everything was really something of a bonus for me. I seemed to get the hang of things fairly quickly and I made it my ambition to stay in the team all season. I got absolutely exhausted at times as I had hardly had a break during the summer and perhaps I should not have played all the way through the season, but I was determined to keep going.

Having at last tasted the thrill of winning my first silverware at senior level, it made me hungry for more and despite being grateful for the forthcoming summer break, I was already looking forward to next season. Before either a rest or the next campaign could be contemplated, there were the Home internationals. and United's close season tour of Swaziland to get out of the way.

Unfortunately for me, one cancelled out the other. The day after our Wembley triumph we had to receive injections for typhus and cholera because of our trip to South Africa and I suffered an adverse reaction, forcing me out of the international fixtures.

*In action during the FA Charity Shield
match with Liverpool, 20th August 1983*

Chapter 5

CEMENTING MY FUTURE
Season 1983-84

Following the trip to Swaziland, where we faced Tottenham twice and the local national side I could at last relax after a hectic, but highly satisfactory season. Despite the whirlwind start to my career, however, there was still some doubt over my future with Manchester United. It was nothing to do with my footballing ability, but because of the club's involvement in the transfer market.

Last season it was Alan Brazil, now it was Charlie Nicholas of Celtic who was linked to United with a fee of £650,00 being bandied about, but the Scot was in no hurry to make up his mind.

In the meantime AC Milan, sensing that such a transfer, if it did indeed materialise, would see me pushed back into Central League football, something that might not be to my liking, were rumoured to be considering a £1.5million move for me.

Much to my surprise it turned out to be no rumour and United did not discourage the Italian's approach. Indeed, they actually accepted their offer. Personally, I had no thoughts on moving abroad and totally rejected the idea, although it did make me wonder what the future held for me at Old Trafford.

> "On the night which saw goalkeeper Pat Jennings claim
> his 100th international cap, it was me who wore the biggest smile
> as the teams left the field at the end of the game
> as I had scored my first international goal."

Some of the critics suggested that I could possibly be a 'one season wonder' and after the opening day of season 1983-84 they might not have been far off the mark, as I had my most undistinguished outing to date in a Manchester United shirt. Looking back, perhaps the transfer talk had affected me more than I had cared to admit at the time.

Against Queen's Park Rangers at Old Trafford, I stabbed an easy shot past the post after only six minutes and some seventy minutes later, with the game poised on a knife edge at 2-1 in our favour, I scorned another scoring opportunity and the chance to secure the points by finishing weakly. Immediately after this half-hearted effort I was substituted for the first time in my career at club level.

The manager refused to go along with the media's talk of "alarm bells ringing" or that I was "tired" and stated that I would keep my place in the side to face Forest two days later. Perhaps a rest would have been better, as Forest inflicted our first home defeat in seventeen months and I was once again ineffective.

I had to wait until our European Cup Winners Cup tie against Dukla Prague before I got the rest many felt I needed, but this was enforced as I was suspended rather than dropped, following my bookings in both games against Valencia last season.

Although manager Ron Atkinson's backing kept my confidence up, it was away from the goldfish bowl environment of Manchester that saw my season suddenly flicker into life. Despite the stuttering start to the season, Billy Bingham had no hesitation in selecting me for Northern Ireland's European Championship qualifying tie against Austria.

Trafford, Manchester

On the night which saw goalkeeper Pat Jennings claim his 100th international cap, it was myself who wore the biggest smile as the teams left the field at the end of the game as I had scored my first international goal. Already 1-0 up, thanks to a 28th minute Billy Hamilton goal, my strike at almost an identical time in the second half paved the way for a memorable victory.

Dispossessing a hesitant Kienast, I sprinted some twenty-five yards, before beating the advancing Koncilla with a low shot from around fifteen yards out. Martin O'Neil added a third in the final minute, after the Austrians had pulled a goal back seven minutes previously.

It took me another couple of weeks before I got off the mark at League level, scoring twice in the 3-3 draw at Carrow Road Norwich. Neither were anything spectacular, mere tap ins to be more exact, but they were goals and part of the encouragement that was required to give me a much needed boost after something of a disappointing start to the season.

Fourteen days later, I was again on the score sheet in the 3-0 victory against West Bromwich Albion, my first goal at Old Trafford for some ten months and the tabloids, who had been carrying much criticism towards me in the past few weeks, were now singing a completely song. 'Whiteside's Super Goal' and 'United's Kid Courage Ends Goal Famine' sprang out from a couple of the back pages.

It had been a long time coming, but it was a goal worth waiting for in more ways than one. The move had began with Arthur Albiston and Ashley Grimes, travelling the length of the pitch, before Ashley crossed the ball into the Albion penalty area. Bustling my way past McNaught and Bennett, I back headed the ball over the outstretched arm of Paul Barron.

Despite returning to something like the form of my early career, transfer speculation was still rife around Old Trafford. Alan Brazil's name was once again floating about, while Andy Gray of cash strapped Wolves was another name mentioned. Neither came to anything, but completely out of the blue, Ron Atkinson signed Garth Crooks from Tottenham on a month's loan, with the possibility of a permanent move at the knockdown price of £150,000. I was now under added pressure to perform to a higher standard and find the back of the net on a more regular basis.

Thankfully, I had little time to worry about the new arrival, as I was off to Hamburg with the Northern Ireland squad to face West Germany. By the end of ninety-minutes, Garth Crooks had more or less been forgotten about, for the time being at least.

With a capacity 61,000 packed into the Volkspark for the group six European Championship qualifier, Northern Ireland shocked the World Cup finalists of the previous year by inflicting their first defeat at the hands of a European side for nine years. One goal was enough to decide the outcome of the game, scored by yours truly.

The goal came five minutes into the second half. A run by Stewart down the left, saw his shot blocked by Schumacher in the West German goal. From the rebound, paul Ramsey disappointingly saw his shot rebound off another German defender, but only as far as me, moving in on goal. Taking the ball in my stride, I drove it firmly past the helpless goalkeeper.

A slight leg knock, the result of some close German attention in Hamburg did not prevent me from declaring myself fit to face Watford at Old Trafford three days later. It was, however, an announcement that I had not needed to make, as a look at the team list after training on the Friday morning revealed that I had been dropped to the substitute's bench, with new recruit Garth Crooks installed in my place.

Terry Butcher challenges me for the ball
during the England v Northern Ireland
Home International Championship match, 4th April 1984

"Norman Whiteside has done tremendously well" Ron Atkinson told the press prior to the game, "but it won't do him any harm to sit back and take stock for a while. I am hoping that the rest that we can give Norman will help provide us with more goals". The manager also dropped hints that he felt that I had been hampered by a recent groin injury.

Needless to say I was disappointed, especially as I felt that I was beginning to return to form. Crooks played well in his debut match against Watford and to complicate matters further for me, Jesper Olsen was signed from Ajax, another forward looking for a permanent first-team spot. The competition was becoming tougher, although Olesn was not really a direct threat. Thankfully it would be the close season before Olsen would appear, giving me a little breathing space and time to force my way back into the team on a regular basis.

I didn't have too long to wait until I reclaimed my place in the United starting line up, as with Garth Crooks cup-tied I was back in the old number ten shirt, partnering my old youth team pal Mark Hughes against Oxford United at the Manor Ground. I had though appeared briefly as substitute the previous Saturday at West Ham, when I almost managed to score during my half hour on the pitch.

I certainly realised that I simply had to fight for my place and I accepted the challenge. But perhaps the enforced rest was what I needed to re-charge the old batteries.

The Milk Cup tie, against manager Ron Atkinson's old club saw Oxford hold us to a 1-1 draw and I was disappointed with my performance, as were most of my team mates. It was particularly frustrating that I could not do more to ensure that we progressed into the next round and also prove to the manager that I should be in his starting line-up in the weeks ahead. Such frustration played a big part in me eventually being booked.

As with the present day, whenever a player is out of the first-team picture for a few games, the newspaper speculation begins to mount as regards to an eventual transfer. Rumour had it that Gianni Rivera, a contact with AC Milan had apparently been told that I was indeed available if his club was interested.

> ## "I didn't have too long to wait until I reclaimed my place in the United starting line up, and I almost managed to score during my half hour on the pitch"

Milan were to deny any interest, while Ron Atkinson said that the club had received no offers for me. At the end of the day, any decision regarding a move would have been mine and at this time it was something that had not entered my mind. It did occur to me, however, that the United hierarchy could consider me to be an eighteen-year-old novice, whose career might stutter along rather than propel me into one of the top players in the country. With any transfer fee going to be over a million, then it would certainly be good business to sell a player who had cost them nothing.

I received encouraging letters from the supporters, who did not want me to go, as the transfer rumours continued to evolve, with Sampdoria's name also appearing on the back pages alongside my name. "Name your price United", one of their officials had reportedly said. The additional carrot of a part-exchange with Trevor Francis or Liam Brady was also mooted.

My British Championship
Winners Medal from May 1984

All the talk of transfer to here, there and everywhere did begin to have something of an unsettling effect, with some of Ron Atkinson's comments in the press not helping much as he did not come out and say that there was no way that he would sell me. So, after much consideration, and feeling somewhat disillusioned, I announced that I would be prepared to talk to any club who were interested in me.

Garth Crooks continued to figure in Ron Atkinson's team selections, but many felt that I contributed more to the overall play and it wasn't until December 21st that I was recalled to the United team, against Stoke City at Old Trafford, a selection that effectively ended the Tottenham man's United loan deal even though it still had just under a month to run.

The scrappy one-goal victory for United did little to help my cause and it was indeed felt that I was fortunate to remain on the pitch for ninety minutes, following a challenge on Hampton. The Stoke man, later in the game, took out some form of retaliation on me and he received his marching orders from the referee. I thought he was a little unlucky, with the tackle clumsy rather than malicious.

Perhaps if I required something to kick-start my career, then it was an appearance in front of the Kop at Anfield. A match against Liverpool was always likely to raise the temperatures and get the old adrenaline bubbling away. Such games were always important to win, but United's chances of remaining in the championship race hinged on the January 2nd meeting. These blood-and-thunder fixtures rarely produced classic encounters, but the atmosphere always compensated for this.

As the 1-1 score line suggests, this was not a match of vintage proportions, with the pitch resembling a battlefield at times. Indeed, Liverpool's 21st minute goal looked for a long time to be the match winner.

We had lost Gordon McQueen with a hamstring injury after twenty minutes, while they had lost Dalglish with a depressed fracture of the cheek. For most of the game, my own contribution to the affair had been a booking for a foul on Sammy Lee. That was, until the dying minutes.

Ray Wilkins, our driving force in midfield due to the absence of Bryan Robson, crossed the ball towards the edge of the Liverpool area. A ball which Nicol failed to clear. Substitute Garth Crooks beat Kennedy to the ball and his header fell invitingly and I had the time and the room to drive the ball left-footed past Grobbelaar. A crucial point was snatched from the jaws of defeat.

The goal not only ensured a point, but also my place in the side, for the immediate future at least.

Having been dumped out of the Milk Cup by Oxford at the third attempt, being drawn against Bournemouth in the 3rd round of the F. A. Cup brought a few shudders through the Old Trafford corridors. They were shudders that were to turn to groans of despair when the third Division side dispatched us out of the competition 3-0. At this point, I would have gladly exchanged the bleak surroundings of Dean Court for the sunshine of Italy.

David Meek (The Manchester Evening News)
"United's Frank Stapleton and Norman Whiteside were dominated by defenders who were no more than bread and butter players."

In the League, we continued to keep our eyes on the top place, but failed to convince the critics that we were worthy of the championship. Since the goal at Anfield, I had failed to score in the following three games, but I suddenly hit a fine

run of form, scoring five goals in five games. In the 2-1 win against Sunderland at Old Trafford on February 25th, the only one of the five, when I did not score, brought some strong criticism from the members of the press for what they considered 'robust play'.

Derek Wallis (The Daily Mirror)
"Whiteside, whose place in the team will be at greatest risk if manager Ron Atkinson ever signs one of the forwards he keeps talking about, used his powerful frame as a battering ram with his elbows more in evidence than usual.
It brought him a reprimand from Sunderland's Gordon Chisholm, who after being booked for fouling Whitside, insisted that the young Irishman had made a meal of it.
He goes in with arms and elbows and everything' complained Chisholm, 'it is just a matter of time before people start having a go back. He can't be allowed to play the way that he does. He's getting away with murder, but the referee did nothing."

Peter Johnson (The Daily Mail)
"You can't play football the Norman Whiteside way and hope to make friends of First Division defenders. It is bruising to the ego as well as to the body to be pushed around by a hard man who, according to his birth certificate, is still a mere youth. There has always been a suspicion that Whiteside has more elbows and hips than the average modern striker and in a season which his place has been constantly threatened by United's ambitions to develop a keener appetite for physical contact. But he has rarely provoked the kind of anger that left Sunderland manager Alan Durban seething at the very mention of his name."

"You can't play football the Norman Whiteside way and hope to make friends of First Division defenders"

Although some of the newspaper correspondents had sharpened their pencils to be critical, the supporters fully endorsed my whole-hearted approach, greeting every tackle, nudge and even blatant foul, with a shout of approval, as if I were a matador toying with a bull in a Spanish arena. Ron Atkinson also did little to extinguish my aggression. Perhaps I was a little impetuous at times, but people did tend to forget that I was after all only eighteen.

With disappointment in the two domestic cup competitions, we were determined to make up for this in the European Cup Winners Cup. Having disposed of Dukla Prague and Spartak Varna in the opening two rounds, we faced much tougher opposition in round three when the draw paired us with Spanish giants Barcelona. Maradona and all.

As we prepared for the first leg in the Spaniard's impressive Nou Camp Stadium, the transfer speculation concerning my move to Italy again raised its head, with AC Milan declaring that they would be sending president Farini to cast an eye over me. I saved them the airfare, as a stomach strain, which had seen me substituted against Aston Villa was enough to keep me out of the tie altogether.

A Graeme Hogg own goal saw United slip behind in the 33rd minute and as the minutes ticked away, it looked as if we had survived a tricky tie with only a one goal deficit. However, thirty seconds from time, the Spaniards struck again, leaving us with an uphill task at Old Trafford.

I missed the following match against Leicester City, but returned to face Arsenal, having something of a quiet game before the big night against Barcelona at Old Trafford. Many felt that United had missed my competitive edge at the Nou Camp, while at the same time hoping that I could contribute in some way to ours attempt at salvaging something from the tie.

Ron Atkinson

"I believe Norman will cause Barcelona a lot of problems. Alesanco, who played against him in the World Cup, will have told his team mates all about him and their defenders will not relish their task against Norman and Frank Stapleton."

As early as the fifteenth minute, in front of a feverent 58,350 Old Trafford crowd, we threatened the Barcelona goal and I came close to opening the scoring. Reacting quickly after a mix up between goalkeeper Urruti and Alesanco, I lobbed the ball towards goal, but could only stand and watch as it hit the top of the crossbar and bounced over. Seven minutes later we did, however, go in front. Frank Stapleton forced a corner on the left and from the Ray Wilkins flag kick my back header was met by Bryan Robson who stooped to head home from close range.

With the crowd totally behind us, we maintained the momentum, but found the Barcelona defence difficult to penetrate and it wasn't until five minutes after the interval that a second goal materialised.

An Alonso back pass caused problems in the visiting defence and as I put the 'keeper under pressure the ball was scrambled away, but only as far as Remi Moses. Snatching the loose ball, our effervescent midfielder quickly sent it back from where it had come. Urruti could then only block Ray Wilkins's shot and before he couldgrab the ball at a second attempt Bryan Robson had put the scores level on aggregate.

Two minutes later we were ahead. Arthur Albiston surged down the left wing and I managed to head his cross to the feet of Frank Stapleton. Quick as a flash, the ball was dispatched into the back of the Spaniard's net. The noise from the crowd was now reaching a deafening level as we fought to hold on to our well earned advantage.

With eighteen minutes to go I was replaced by Mark Hughes, as I began to tire, but I was more than satisfied with my contribution to the game. One that still ranks alongside Old Trafford's most memorable encounters.

My see-saw season had brought me much frustration, both on and off the pitch, with some of the former landing me in bother with match officials. As the campaign moved into its final few weeks, I was walking a disciplinary tightrope with a total of sixteen points. One further booking would bring me an automatic one-match ban. With an outside chance of the Championship I certainly did not want to jeopardise this, so I had to try and curtail my aggressive tendencies. Bookings in Europe also had to be avoided, as we faced Juventus in the semi-finals of the Cup Winners Cup and a pair of cautions would mean missing the final if we got through.

In the first leg tie against the Italian giants at Old Trafford, we were without both Ray Wilkins and Bryan Robson, so extra responsibility fell on my shoulders. Juventus, inspired by the likes of Rossi, Platini and Boniek took advantage of our lightweight midfield and took a fifteen minute lead. With John Gidman already off injured, the pressure was indeed on, but the volume from the fifty eight odd thousand was turned up when my point blank shot rebounded off Tacconi giving substitute Alan Davies the opportunity to score.

I could have become the hero of the night if I had not shunned a scoring opportunity at the near post late in the game. Frank Stapleton had missed a similar chance earlier in the second half. We faced an uphill struggle in the Turin second leg in Turin.

Michele Platini's swapped Juventus shirt. The best player I ever played against

A 1-0 defeat at Notts County in the following game did little to help our Championship cause, nor did a 0-0 draw at Watford. From the high expectations of a few weeks ago, we were now looking at disappointment. Not only did those one hundred and eighty minutes alter our title hopes, they also cost me my place in the team in the next fixture against Coventry City at Old Trafford. Having failed to score since March 3rd, seven games ago.

With the return against Juventus looming, losing my place was the last thing I wanted, as it is everyone's ambition to play in a major European Final. A good performance in Italy could also help my cause if ever I fancied the mega money transfer that had been mentioned in the press in the past.

> ## "Our Cup Winners Cup final dream was cruelly shattered by an injury time goal from Juventus' Rossi."

Amid a cauldron of red flares and thunderous firecrackers, with Bryan Robson again missing and Mark Hughes playing in my place, we only managed to hold out for thirteen minutes before the home side took the inevitable lead through Boniek. We bravely kept the Italians at bay, but rarely threatened their goal and with the game moving into the last half hour I was called into the action, replacing Frank Stapleton.

Eight minutes later, it looked as if the manager's decision had paid dividends, as I pounced to score with a left foot shot high into the net, after a Paul McGrath effort was blocked. With extra time looming, our dream was cruelly shattered by an injury-time goal from Rossi.

The goal did not earn me a re-call to the starting line up, Mark Hughes retained his place as our title challenge fizzled out and I failed to make the starting line-up for any of the final six games.

I look on as three great players fight for the ball

Chapter 6

RE-CAPTURING MY OLD FORM
Season 1984-85

Season 1983-84 had ended on a wave of disappointment as I watched my youth-team mate Mark Hughes overtake me in the pecking order. As the following season drew near I found myself under further pressure when the manager signed Gordon Strachan from Aberdeen and long term target Alan Brazil from Tottenham Hotspur. Although the ginger-headed Scot was not a direct threat to me, he was another addition to the squad and another player who wanted a permanent place in the side.

Determined to put the disappointment of the signings behind me, I buckled down to pre-season training, maintaining the self-belief that if I kept working away at The Cliff training ground then first team football was sure to return. Perhaps luck was something that had passed me by in the latter stages of season 1983-84, but as the pre-season preparations began to intensify, I received a welcome boost.

A close-season knee operation to Frank Stapleton failed to heal as quickly as expected, with the first team door opening to me for the pre-season friendlies at least, allowing me the opportunity of staking a claim for the early League fixtures.

"It was obvious to both myself and the United faithful that I was beginning to recapture something like my old form"

Three starts and a substitute appearance in the six friendlies was all that came my way prior to the big kick off and for the opening fixture, against Watford at Old Trafford, a place on the substitutes bench was all that came my way.

Chelsea's visit to Manchester on September 5th, with United still looking for their first win, saw Ron Atkinson decide to gamble on a rather youthful attack, pairing Mark Hughes and myself up front. It had been some eleven months since I had scored at Old Trafford, so there was considerable pressure on me. Not just to score, but to hit it off with Sparky.

Sadly, United once again failed to secure both points, as former United player Micky Thomas cancelled out Jesper Olsen's first United goal after fifteen minutes. A goal I set up with a timely chip into the area. I did come close on a couple of occasions, with both shots hitting the side netting. The Hughes/Whiteside partnership continued three days later at Newcastle and once again my contribution was setting up a goal. Another pass resulted in Arthur Albiston being brought down for a penalty.

It was obvious to both myself and the United faithful that I was beginning to recapture something like my old form and alongside my new sidekick, Mark Hughes, I was shrugging off the disappointment of the previous months.

The journey to Highfield Road, Coventry, on September 15th saw United score their eighth goal in two games as well as bringing to an end my personal goal drought, with a double strike in the 43rd and 64th minutes. Although Mark Hughes failed to score on this particular occasion, the junior striking partnership, rivals for a long-term place in the United line-up, had renewed their shoulder to shoulder acquaintance with unquestionable enthusiasm. A pairing that had first smouldered in the United junior sides not too long ago.

Mark Hughes
"We seemed to hit it off together straight away. Somehow, we complemented each other and it seems we have never lost the knack. Although Norman is a year younger than me, I've always learned from him. That's why, when he beat me into the first team, it did not worry me. It was always recognised at Old Trafford that he was...well, something special".

Wembley bound?

It was Sparky, however, who maintained the challenge for first-team football, scoring in the UEFA cup tie against Raba Gyor, before adding a hat trick in the 4-0 League Cup win against Burnley. In the latter of the two, I was replaced by Alan Brazil, as I had suffered a knock to the knee. An injury that was to see the name of Norman Whiteside omitted from the United team sheet until early November, returning against PSV Eindhoven in the UEFA Cup.

The injury set off an early scare that I would have to under go an exploratory operation, but this was quickly dismissed and I was more than pleased to get back into match action against the Dutch side, coming on in place of Frank Stapleton in our 1-0 win. During my spell on the touch line, I just had to grit my teeth, as I knew that at this level and with the squad that we had, you could not afford to be on the sidelines for too long. You really had to move heaven and hell to get back into the side.

Three days later, I replaced Jesper Olsen against Leicester City and against Luton Town on November 17th I was in the starting line-up in place of Alan Brazil.

I rewarded the boss by scoring both goals in our 2-0 victory. The first, one minute after the interval finished off a five man move, brushing aside team-mate Jesper Olsen to shoot past two Luton defenders on the goal line. The second, six minutes from time, was a crisp left foot drive that beat my Northern Ireland team-mate, and stand in Luton goalkeeper, Mal Donaghy, propelling me back into the tabloid headlines.

Although happy to be back amongst the goals, I was a bit critical of myself, proclaiming that I should have had a hat-trick, as I put a header against the bar. I simply had to keep the momentum going, as there were four players chasing two positions. Perhaps my first goal against Luton brought a few upraised eyebrows, as I thrust aside Jesper as he was poised to latch onto the ball, but it would not have mattered who it was, as I had blinkers on. I was going to have that goal no matter what.

Those goals, my first since September 15th were to be my last until February 23rd, did little to alter many opinions that I was little more than a Joe Jordan clone. At times more concerned about the physical side of the game than attempting to improve my footballing skills and increase my rather moderate goal return. Having achieved so much, so early in my career, match-winning performances were expected on a regular basis.

A hamstring injury against Norwich City on December 11th gave my plans for the months ahead a serious jolt, just as seemed to have regained something like my old form. By the time I had returned on January 26th, for the FA Cup tie against Coventry City at Old Trafford, United had enjoyed mixed fortunes. Losing five and winning four of the nine games.

I returned to the first team line up for a friendly against Oldham Athletic, but in the rather unfamiliar position of midfield. I much preferred a striking role, but you can't complain about any role you are given in a team like United. It was simply great to back in action.

They reckon that every now and again everyone gets a lucky break and I certainly got one prior to the cup-tie against Coventry, when Frank Stapleton went down with 'flu. Although I did not exactly turn in a match-winning performance, in the 2-1 win, it was enough to keep me in the side the following Saturday. In fact, my good luck continued for the remainder of the season, as my name was only missing from the United team-sheet once.

However, when Frank returned, against his former club Arsenal, I was relegated to the substitute's bench and to say that I was unhappy about it is an understatement. My frustration and disappointment, however, was soon to be forgotten as

I was called upon to replace Kevin Moran after only fourteen minutes. By the end of the afternoon, I had the biggest smile in north London, as I scored the only goal of the game, controlling Jesper Olsen's through ball before hitting a left-foot drive into the back of the net from the edge of the Arsenal penalty area.

That goal kept our Championship hopes alive, as did the 1-1 draw against Everton seven days later. A missed Gordon Strachan penalty could have seen the points doubled, but on the other hand, Gary Bailey's penalty save from Kevin Sheedy prevented a possible setback. While the manager was not exactly spoilt for choice, I was given a place in the starting line up, but with Mark Hughes and Alan Brazil also included, I found myself shoring up the midfield alongside Mike Duxbury.

My enthusiastic, rather than majestic, performance clearly unsettled the Toffee's, with Peter Reid eventually receiving a booking for a retaliationary foul on me. If my presence unsettled Peter and his Everton team mates, it must have driven the West Ham United players and their supporters insane the following Saturday, in our 6th round F. A. Cup tie.

"Wonderful Whiteside" and The Hit Man" were just two of the headlines that appeared after the match, as United strode to their 15th post war F. A. Cup semi-final with a 4-2 win in a memorable encounter, which saw me score my first senior hat-trick.

To their credit, West Ham had asked for a postponement of the tie due to an outbreak of influenza, but they were forced to play by the Football Association and had to field a weakened side. Perhaps if the F. A. had been aware that I was to inflict further suffering on the Hammers, then they would have probably been a little more tolerant.

It was Mark Hughes who gave us the lead in the 21st minute, with a left foot shot, but a Graeme Hogg own goal fifteen minutes later put the visitors back into the game. Giving as good as they got, discarding the flu bug from their minds, West Ham certainly looked capable of snatching a draw. That was until six minutes prior to the interval when I scored the first of my hat trick.

A Gordon Strachan corner, delayed momentarily while police gave the Scot some cover after being hit by a coin as he prepared to take his kick, was headed forward by Paul McGrath. With my back to goal, I managed to stretch and head the ball past McAllister in the Hammers goal.

Number two came in the 75th minute, following a free kick from Graeme Hogg, which he drove deep towards the West Ham goal. Once again I managed to get to it, with the ball deflecting off my leg and into the net, as the 'keeper dived in the opposite direction, caught out by my sudden intervention.

"With West Ham forced to play by the Football Association, I was about to inflict further suffering on the Hammers"

At 3-1, the tie looked to have been decided, but our supporters began nervously looking at their watches, afetr Paul Allen narrowed the score line to 3-2 with four minutes still to play. With thoughts of a replay drifting around Old Trafford, play became a bit more cautious, but the result was put beyond all doubt three minutes from time.

Moving into the Hammers penalty area, Gordon Strachan was fouled by Paul Brush and having previously taken over the penalty kick responsibilities from the ginger haired Scot, I not only notched my first senior hat trick, but converted my first United penalty.

A hat-trick at any time is rewarding, but having not exactly enjoyed the best of seasons, the triple strike was particularly pleasing, perhaps more so as it was from my "new" midfield role. As I have said before, it didn't matter where I played, as long as I was involved. Playing deeper is a lot different from being up front, but the boss gave me instructions to hit the opposition penalty box as often as possible and it worked out fine against West Ham.

I found it hard work running up and down, but it began to do wonders for my fitness and I enjoyed the challenge. What happens when Bryan Robson returns, I don't know.

As for taking the penalties, I didn't mind the responsibility and if I were honest, I would say that I enjoyed it. It was the first one that I had taken at any level.

Wembley was now only one step away, with Liverpool standing in our way. But before the titanic semi-final battles, we had a few important League fixtures to fulfil.

On the back of the West Ham cup victory, Mark Hughes and I scored the goals that gave United the points in a tempestuous fixture at White Hart Lane, but the following week I had to leave the pitch rather prematurely against West Ham due to a knee injury. Fortunately, it was nothing serious and I was able to play in the next fixture against Villa, when I scored again. I took my total to eight for the season in our 5-0 win over Stoke City, the week before the Liverpool cup tie at Goodison Park.

The sports pages seemed to concentrate on nothing else but the cup tie during the days leading up to it, with the love/hate relationship between United and Liverpool a regular feature. My own reputation received just as much coverage.

I was quick to point out that most of the talk was related to my tackling, but it seemed to matter little that I received just as much, if not more than I gave out. I never ever complained about such treatment, as I thought it rather unprofessional that one player should have a go at another off the park. I was always encouraged to tackle hard and I readily admit that I would get stuck in during a game.

I know a lot of people went around calling me 'dirty', but I never looked at it that way. I never went out to "do" a rival in a tackle, as my disciplinary record showed. Up until that point, only one player has ever had to leave the field due to one of my tackles. I went in totally committed, but never to deliberately hurt anyone.

In the semi-final, if Liverpool had any advantage, it was playing the tie on Merseyside, a short distance across Stanley Park from their Anfield home. United had little to fear and in many eyes, even outside the confines of Manchester 16, we were favourites to win the famous old trophy.

After a somewhat dour and uneventful opening forty-five minutes and despite my earlier protestations in the press regarding my style of play, I was involved in an early tussle with Sammy Lee.

Play tended to get bogged down at times, but it was United who took the lead through Mark Hughes in the 69th minute. An inswinging corner from Gordon Strachan was headed on by Graeme Hogg and Bryan Robson was on hand to deflect the ball goalwards, but it was a flick of Sparkie's heel that propelled the ball past Grobbelaar.

As the minutes ticked away, we held on to our lead and it looked as if we were Wembley bound. However, with only three minutes remaining, Neal and Lee combined to give Whelan possession out on the wing and not having learned our

1985 FA Cup Final shirt

lesson from the Milk Cup Final of 1983, we allowed the Republic of Ireland international the time to send a right-footed shot past Gary Bailey to ensure extra time.

The additional thirty minutes took a similar path to the initial ninety, with United taking the lead eight minutes into the extra time. A low twenty-yard drive from Frank Stapleton taking a deflection off Whelan and beating Grobbelaar.

Once again we felt that we were on the verge of victory, but thirty seconds from the end, Liverpool once again snatched something from the jaws of defeat, when all seemed lost. Dalglish, as always a torment, crossed and Rush headed the ball over the outstretched arms of Gary Bailey. Paul Walsh, dashing in prodded the ball over the line. 2-2 and a replay at Maine Road four days later.

"My temperament was severely tested at Southampton by former Liverpool player Jimmy Case"

In Manchester, the pace was slightly more up tempo than it had been at Goodison., with Bryan Robson and myself constantly harrying the Liverpool midfield, while at the same time attempting to create opportunities for our forwards. Amid some frantic challenges, Kenny Dalglish found his name in the referee's notebook following an overzealous challenge on yours truly just before the interval. By that time, Liverpool were actually in front, thanks to a deflected Paul McGrath header.

Within sixty seconds of the restart, we were level. Robbo played a one two with Mark Hughes before scoring with a tremendous twenty-five-yard shot. From then on, Ron Atkinson's half-time pep talk was strictly adhered to as we kept pressurising the Liverpool defence, ensuring that there was only going to be one winner. Thirteen minutes later, we got the break we needed.

With the Liverpool defence looking for an offside flag that was never likely to appear, Sparky ran on to Gordon Strachan's through ball before sending a rasping shot high into the net from the edge of the penalty area. From then on there was never going to be a repeat of the Goodison Park encounter and we held our lead. We were Wembley bound.

With Saturday May 18th outlined in red ink in my diary, you would have thought that the remaining League fixtures would have been approached in a slightly more leisurely fashion, especially when fellow Wembley finalists Everton were more or less Champions elect, ten points ahead of us with only six fixtures remaining.

For some, the rather meaningless games would have been played with one eye on the final, but for me, there was only one way to play football and that was to give your all in every game. Sometimes though this was not enough, as in front of the smallest attendance for a live televised game, 10,320, Luton Town well and truly ended our Championship challenge with a 2-1 victory. My close-range shot had put us back in the game at 1-1, but a booking, six minutes from the end, was all that I had to show for my afternoon's exertions.

My frustration at losing the Championship was also in evidence in the following fixture against Southampton at Old Trafford and my temperament was severely tested by former Liverpool player Jimmy Case, now playing for the South Coast club. A booking for a foul on me soon quietened him down a bit though.

Here I am celebrating my extra-time match winning goal in the 1985 FA Cup Final

Thoughts of pre Cup Final injuries never crossed my mind and I once again covered every blade of Old Trafford grass, left Mark Dennis (himself no novice in the tough-tackling stakes) limping, while also hitting the visitors' bar with one of our few attempts on goal in the 0-0 draw.

Jimmy Case (Southampton)
"He has an awful lot to learn. He is sly on the field and he is getting away with it particularly in home games because he is playing for Manchester United. I know how playing for a really big club can give you added protection. I was never suspended until I left Liverpool. Clubs like that, give you a shroud of protection.
I'm not saying that Norman is a bad player. He has obvious attributes. If he resorts to his physique to win challenges fairly and squarely, no one will complain. But he is definitely getting himself earmarked by other players because some things he does are absolutely blatant. What he must learn above everything is to concentrate on his own game and not on upsetting other people. I learned that myself when I was younger, but I was never as blatant as Whiteside. People in the game don't like what Norman Whiteside is doing. I'm afraid, at present, he is being a bit of a bugger."

Our FA Cup Final opponents took the championship and our hopes of preventing them from clinching a League and Cup double were dealt something of a blow in our final League match of the season against Watford at Vicarage Road, a few miles up the road from Wembley, when we suffered a 5-1 drubbing. Our first defeat in six games.

Brian Clough (Nottingham Forest manager)
"I'm not sure whether Whiteside is talented or not, but I hope he realises that millions of starry eyed kids will be watching his every move. But he is there, in the middle of our show piece on Saturday, privileged and meeting royalty beforehand.
"I hope the millions are switching off their television sets at 4.40pm and saying, what a mature young man he's become."

Appearing in a FA Cup Final at Wembley is every footballer's dream. An occasion to savour and remember for the rest of your life. I was fortunate that this was my second. They are, at times, non-events though, with the build up and whatever often overshadowing the actual ninety minutes. The 1985 Cup Final was no outstanding match and was to stretch from the normal hour-and-a-half into a further enduring thirty minutes of extra time.

Peter Reid, who was suddenly caught in two minds, collected a misplaced pass by Paul McGrath, almost mid way inside our half. He could pass to team-mate Andy Gray wide to his left, or attempt to go it alone. Taking the latter option, he pushed the ball forward towards our goal.

Alert to the immediate danger, Kevin Moran launched himself towards the man and the ball, but unfortunately for all concerned, it was the former that he made contact with. Moments later, after much pushing and shoving, a distraught Moran was escorted towards the touchline, sent off by referee Peter Willis. The first player to be sent off in a Wembley Cup Final. With ten men, the odds were now even less in our favour and you wouldn't have bet against Everton winning the double. But when Willis blew for full time, neither goalkeeper had been beaten.

Into extra time and ten minutes from the end of the additional thirty, came the decisive moment.

Jesper Olsen collected the ball just inside our half, found Mark Hughes inside the centre circle, as the weary legs of both teams struggled across the energy sapping Wembley turf. Sparky, moving across the pitch from left to right, threaded the ball through to me as my well timed run beat the Everton offside trap.

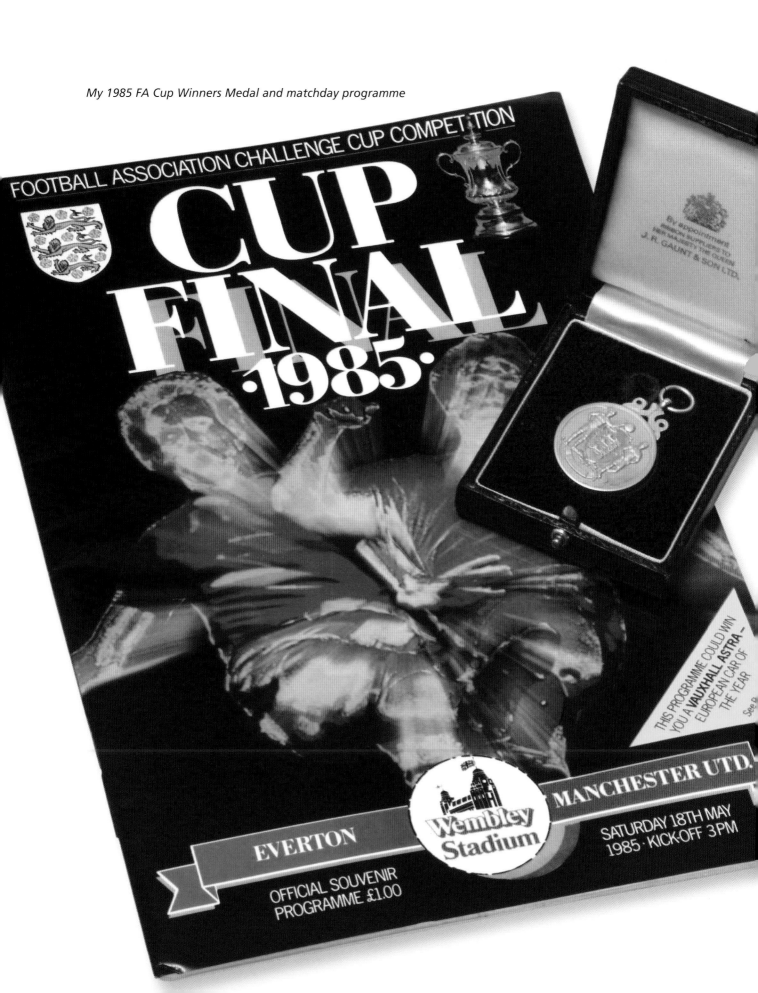

My 1985 FA Cup Winners Medal and matchday programme

David Lacey (The Guardian)
"Van den Hauwe seemed to have covered the danger, but Whiteside threw him off balance by waggling his left foot over the ball. He then used the left back as a screen, as with the same foot, he curled a shot towards the inside of the far post. Fully sighted, Southall might have made the save, but Whiteside's clever concealment of the shot meant that he took off a fraction too late to stop it."

Jeff Powell (The Daily Mail)
"It was a goal worthy of winning any Final and one made all the more poignant by Southall's earlier save at the feet of the same United player.

The electric scoreboard, which had read in error most of the afternoon – Everton 0 Manchester United 70, made a flickering adjustment to 0-1 as the day was done."

It was a tremendous feeling watching the ball curl into the net and particularly pleasing as it was something that I practised every day in training. There could not have been a better time or place for it to come off. I saw Neville Southall clinging to his near post and worked a situation so that he couldn't see what was happening as Pat Van den Hauwe screened him. I've never felt better in my life than when the ball bent around big Nev because it was the toughest chance after I had missed two others.

The first opportunity struck Southall's shoulder as I tried to clip it over him, but the other was just down to tired legs. The worst part was that if I had dummied the cross then Robbo or two or three others might have scored. After that, I lay flat out, absolutely shattered, for thirty seconds. Luckily it all worked out for us in the end.

> ## "It was a tremendous feeling watching the ball curl into the net - it was something that I practised every day in training"

Ron Atkinson
"Full marks to Norman for a superb goal, but you come to expect something like that from him at Wembley."

Looking back, it was a goal and a Cup Winner's medal that might never have materialised, as earlier in the season it looked as if I was just not going to have a part in Manchester United's challenge. I was really glad that I had decided to roll up my sleeves and get stuck in. I certainly made the correct decision.

The reported Italian interest in me, which had simmered throughout the season, but had faded somewhat in recent months was once again brought to the fore following the events at Wembley and also by my return to form at League level.

Top Italian sides such as AC Milan were unable to try and tempt me away from Manchester due to a transfer ban on imports, but no such regulations applied to newly promoted sides such as Bari. I was considered a prime target for their new challenge.

Thankfully, and much to my relief, the manager, who perhaps could have been tempted to part with me a few months earlier, was quick to state that he was not interested in doing business. This certainly reassured me about my immediate future as I set off to Trinidad and Jamaica with my United team-mates for a two-match tour, before enjoying a well earned break away from the game.

The Manchester United Supporters YEAR BOOK 1985~1986

The 1985-1986
Manchester United Yearbook

Chapter 7

THE HARD MAN
Season 1985-86

As the new season appeared on the horizon, the club received a £1.3 million bid for my services from Lecce. This was rejected by the United board and in an effort to keep me from considering such tempting offers, they offered me an improved contract.

Ron Atkinson
"Norman is an important part of our plans and there is no way we will consider selling him. It is not our policy to sell our best players unless we can bring in replacements and make a substantial amount of money for the club as well."

Returning from a well earned break, I endured the rigours of pre-season training with a spring in my step and following the usual run of the mill friendlies and the FA Charity Shield against Everton at Wembley it was down to the bread and butter of league football once again.

I managed to start the campaign with a goal, scoring our first in a 4-0 win over Aston Villa at Old Trafford with a header in the 46th minute. But, as luck would have it, I only managed to find the net another three times in the First Division (once in the League and twice in the Football League Cup) despite missing only five fixtures.

The second of the five, against Oxford United on September 7th at Old Trafford, the first in a 3-0 win, was up there amongst the best I have scored. Certainly, it was the best I had scored at Old Trafford.

Denis Lowe (The Daily Telegraph)
"Picking the ball up at half way, from a short Bryan Robson pass, Whiteside thrust past Hebberd, Trewick and Briggs in a determined run which ended with a powerful left footed shot which sped inside the far upright."

Bryan Robson
"It was a goal that had everything the fans expect in excitement. The run and finishing were brilliant. I haven't seen better."

"what the chairman offered me was not exactly what I had in mind and was not really what I wanted"

All my appearances were in the number four shirt and being confined to midfield meant I didn't get into the opposition penalty area as often as I would have liked.

Despite my inactivity on the goal front, United stormed off into one of their best ever starts, with ten straight victories. The record-breaking run coming to an end at Luton, when the home side sneaked a 1-1 draw. Although happy with the start, I was not too happy about the proposed new contract that was put my way.

I was not in any real hurry to sign, as I still had about a year to run on my present one, but what the chairman offered me was not exactly what I had in mind and was not really what I wanted. I suppose, I was quite happy to keep United dangling on a string, while allowing me to consider anything that came my way from any other club's.

United, however, must have read my mind as they took the initiative and offered me a new five year, £60,000 a year, deal. This offered me a substantial increase and put me up alongside the highest earners. It was just the type of deal I was after and I happily signed to secure my immediate future.

Northern Ireland 1986 World Cup Shirt

The money was nice, but I really wanted a bag full of medals before I retired. I would be only twenty-five by the time the contract finished and would have eight years experience behind me. So, if I still fancied a shot at football abroad then I would be young enough to give it a try.

The contract was certainly a boost to my career, but an even bigger boost came following an injury to Bryan Robson, when I was named as captain, leading the team out for the first time against Norwich City at Old Trafford in a Screen Sports Super Cup tie. I responded to the honour with United's equalising goal from the penalty spot in the 1-1 draw.

Everything in the garden, however, was not rosy, as I was to endure a rather nightmare ninety minutes against Arsenal four days before Christmas. The Gunners inflicting our first home defeat of the season, with a Charlie Nicholas goal, snatched in the 75th minute. For the stand-in captain, it was not just a defeat, but one that I could perhaps have prevented, had I scored with a 21st minute penalty kick.

To be completely honest, it was more like a pass back than a penalty kick and after the game I relinquished my spot-kick responsibilities. I was not in the least bit worried who took them after that, as long it was one of the other ten.

In our defence of the FA Cup, we dispatched lowly Rochdale in the third round without any real problem's, but against Sunderland in round four things did not go quite so smoothly. At Roker Park, Bryan Robson, upon his return to his native north-east, was sent off during the 0-0 draw. In the replay, we won comfortably enough, 3-0, but after the match, Dave Swindlehurst accused me of deliberately punching him as we challenged for a high ball.

David Swindlehurst (Sunderland)
"We both went for a high ball, when he suddenly swung his arm back and whacked me with the back of his fist. He caught me right in the eyeball. There was no need for it. The pain was terrific and I couldn't see out of the eye for the rest of the match.

I know Whiteside has a bit of a reputation for being a tough customer and you are always a little bit wary of him. But this was completely unexpected and I was struggling to see the ball afterwards. The thing that most disappointed me was that it happened right in front of the referee and he did nothing about it."

Perhaps I did catch him, but it was certainly not intentional and as the referee did not book me, he must have thought the same. If I had been booked, it would have taken me over the twenty point mark, resulting in aa automatic two-match ban, so it was a bit of a relief.

The relief though did not last for long, as I was booked in the following game, a 2-1 defeat against West Ham. I was uncertain at first if I had indeed been booked, but the referee confirmed after the match that he booked me for "ungentlemanly conduct".

I was disappointed by the booking and by the furore that it seemed to cause. My every tackle or challenge seemed to be put under the microscope, but at least the suspense of waiting was over and I was banned. People were saying that I was a dirty player, but the bookings were not for bad fouls. I was disappointed with the last one, as it was for retaliation and to lose as well made it a bad day, denting our title hopes.

My last game before the suspension was against Liverpool at Anfield and we had something of a lucky escape. Not in the 1-1 draw, but before the game itself.

*Northern Ireland Penant
from the 1986 World Cup*

As the United team coach pulled up outside Anfield, the waiting crowd surged forward as the players began to disembark. Suddenly, without warning, amid a hail of bottles and stones, someone released a spray of chemical gas. Clayton Blackmore took the brunt of it, but twenty-four people required hospital treatment.

As it had done for much of the past nineteen years, Manchester United's title challenge stuttered to a halt long before the eventual honours were decided. One of the reasons was the decision to sell Mark Hughes to Barcelona.

"At the end of the season, there was to be no relaxing break, as I was off to Mexico to play in my second World Cup Finals"

The deal had been agreed in January and after that Sparky failed to find the back of the net for two months, having scored ten times up until that point. It was rather surprising that United decided to let him go, after turning down offers for me. Could he do without Sparky more than he could me?

As my former youth-team colleague prepared to pack his bags, I celebrated my twenty-first birthday, even though I felt like something of a veteran. At an age when many are just breaking into first team football, I had all the trappings offered to a top footballer. Luxuries such as a £200,000 five-bedroom house complete with its own snooker room, a top-of-the-range car complete with telephone and a five-year big money deal with Manchester United.

At the end of the season, there was to be no relaxing break, or a trip to Singapore, Bangkok and Hong Kong with United, as I was off in the opposite direction, to Mexico to play in my second World Cup Finals. This time, however, there was to be no entries into the record books or notable performances, as Northern Ireland found themselves drawn into a really difficult group.

Alongside us in the Guadalajara based Group 4 were Algeria, Spain and Brazil, with the former being the only side that we honestly thought that we had a chance against.

As it turned out, they were, and we managed a 1-1 draw against them, for our only point of the tournament. I opened the scoring after six minutes, but Algeria, who had caused upsets in Spain four years previously by defeating both West Germany and Chile, equalised on the hour mark to snatch a point.

Against Spain, we found ourselves a goal behind in the first minute and never really recovered, going 2-0 down before the game was twenty minutes old. A goal mouth scramble saw us pull a goal back a minute after the interval, but we just could not force an equaliser, let alone the two goals needed to snatch a victory.

Having failed to take full points from any of the other two games, there was little hope of us beating Brazil and as it turned out, in a rather lacklustre performance by the South Americans and an even more nondescript one from ourselves, we lost 3-0 and headed for home.

As it was, the finals were more memorable for Pat Jennings's world record 119th cap, against Brazil, on his 41st birthday and Maradona's 'Hand of God' goal against England.

Memories of my international games

Chapter 8
INJURY NIGHTMARES
Season 1986-87

The disappointment of the Mexico World Cup came to a head when I had to return to Manchester for knee surgery. Following the operation, when I felt like a cripple, I had to replan my pre-season schedule as I had been forced to rest up after the operation and when I started pre-season training our physiotherapist, Jimmy McGregor, had to show me how to run again.

I was quite low at this point and could certainly have broken my strictly imposed 'no swearing' vow, something I had not done for over twenty years. I feared the worst, but Jimmy managed to keep me going and got me back into shape. I managed two tough practise matches within forty-eight hours and was soon eager to get back into first-team action.

My fitness was enough to earn me selection for the opening match, but the season got off to a bad start at Highbury, where we lost 1-0 and it wasn't until the fifth fixture that we recorded our first victory, 5-1 against Southampton at Old Trafford, when I scored my second goal, after finding the net the previous week at Leicester.

Our performances were rather poor, winning only three of our opening thirteen and we soon found ourselves at the wrong end of the table, with the manager coming in for quite a bit of criticism. A lot of this, was due to his decision to play me, with many suggesting that I was struggling in some of the games. I would have been the first to admit that I didn't feel 100 per cent, with the knee still not quite right, but the rumours were beginning to circulate that the injury was threatening my career.

"The rumours were beginning to circulate that the injury was threatening my career"

On November 4th, we travelled to Southampton for a League Cup tie, after having drawn 0-0 at Old Trafford and it was a match that was to have dire consequences. There was to be no repeat of the five-star performance of a few weeks earlier, as the Saints won comfortably 4-1. It was another match, that as captain, left me very disappointed, even though I had left the field injured after thirty minutes.

Two days later, Ron Atkinson was sacked, with Alex Ferguson moving into the hot seat twenty-four hours later. One of the reason's given for Big Ron's departure was that 'he had lost the respect of the players', but I had no real complaints about the man who had given me my opportunity at League level. I was even one of only four players who attended his 'farewell party' at his Rochdale home.

Big Ron was so laid back, it was unbelievable at times how relaxed things were. There were never any cross words exchanged and he practically let you do what you liked between Sunday and Friday, as long as you contributed to the game on a Saturday afternoon. Perhaps that is why we were not a bit more successful at League level.

Ron didn't just want to be the manger, he wanted to be a friend of the players as well and again this was perhaps a bad thing. But, at the end of the day, he did create an entertaining side at Old Trafford and you have to wonder, if it wasn't for injuries to key players, if he could have taken United that one step on to the Championship.

My first manager at United, Dave Sexton, had been completely different again. Like Billy Bingham, he was a lovely man, but Dave was very quiet and reserved at times. He was also a real football man, with an in-depth knowledge of the game. Perhaps his tactics were not favoured by many at Old Trafford, but as a person, he is held high in my esteem.

Part of my collection of Northern Ireland caps

1989-90

1987-88

1986-87

1983-84

1985-86

1982-83

1981-82

1984

I still remember that during one of my early spells in hospital with an injury, Dave took the time to come and visit me. It was something completely out of the blue and an act that meant a lot to me at the time. I suppose it really summed up the gentleman that he was.

Alex Ferguson's arrival at Old Trafford caused some concern amongst the senior players at Old Trafford, as we were totally uncertain as to what to expect from the Scot. Gordon Strachan, a player under Fergie at Aberdeen, enlightened us to the sometime's fiery Scot's behaviour. The rather easy life that we had under Ron Atkinson was about to come to an abrupt end.

I was unavailable for selection by the new manager due to injury and it was not until December 7th, that I was able to abandon the treatment table for place in the first team. The manager was still assessing the squad that he had inherited before he made any wholesale changes.

Alex Ferguson
"I have been really impressed by Norman since I came here. He has proved that he can operate up front at a high level and we haven't too many alternatives. When I first saw Norman on the training ground at The Cliff, I felt the excitement that is felt by watching a player of the highest class. I knew about him as a prodigy who had been introduced to the Northern Ireland team at the age of seventeen, and had seen him play at the World Cup finals in Mexico, but I would never have appreciated how good he was without the advantage of studying him at close quarters.
He had self assurance that was extraordinary in a twenty-one year old, the excellence of his technique gave him easy masterly of the ball and he had the gift of making time for himself that is a stamp of quality. No matter how fast the game was or how much pressure was on him, he was an island of composure, looking up and unhurriedly making his decisions. He rarely surrendered possession and he increased the angle and weight of his passes so well that the receiver never had to fight the ball. His eyes were as cold as steel and he had a temperament to match."

I came through a reserve match unscathed and I was ready and raring to go, aiming to make the same sort of impression on the new manager. I was also unconcerned were I played, but I was beginning to consider midfield as my permanent position. However, if the manager wanted to play me up front then that was fine by me.

So against Tottenham Hotspur at Old Trafford I made my first appearance for Alex Ferguson and back in my old forward position I showed that I had not lost my touch, opening the scoring in the 11th minute, of what was a 3-3 draw. I scored again the following week against Aston Villa and made it three goals in four games a fortnight later.

That third strike, which gave United a 1-0 win, was no ordinary goal, nor was it scored in just any old game. The Boxing Day goal secured United both points in the tension filled, volatile fixture against Liverpool at Anfield and it saw me re-claim pole position as public enemy No 1 on the red side of Stanley Park. Alex Ferguson had brought Frank Stapleton back for this game, moved me back into midfield, with Bryan Robson reverting to a more defensive role.

United's Anfield record was second to none, four wins and three draws in the last seven fixtures and I was more than happy to extend this, but my opportunity to do so did not surface until the 78th minute. A Robbo free kick was headed on by Frank Stapleton, but Peter Davenport saw his shot blocked. Jesper Olsen, however, reacted quickest and passed the ball inside to me and I beat Grobbelaar from fifteen yards.

Alex Ferguson's arrival at Old Trafford had certainly blown away the cobwebs that had gathered during the latter days of Ron Atkinson's reign. Making quick, early decisions, training had been stepped up, discipline and personal appearance were paid more attention to. He was certainly out to make his mark early on.

The new year failed to bring immediate good fortune my way. A groin injury, sustained against Newcastle United during the 4-1 New Year's Day victory at Old Trafford, a game in which I scored our second goal, forced me off the pitch one minute after the interval. At least it wasn't as life threatening as that sustained by Kevin Moran.

My former fellow lodger, who flinched at nothing, collided with David McCreery in the 64th minute and fell to the ground unconscious, swallowing his tongue in the process. Only the quick thinking of Jimmy McGregor prevented a serious incident.

My own minor injury did not produce a prolonged period on the side lines and I was back to cause havoc nine days later against Manchester City in the third round of the FA Cup. In the build up to the cup-tie, I was restricted to only light work outs at the Cliff, but I still made the starting line-up, declaring myself fit and my presence clearly unsettling City. There was not much between the two sides as the match progressed and it was not until the sixty-sixth minute that a breakthrough was achieved. Beginning a move in my own half, I followed the play downfield and as Peter Davenport went down under a tackle from White, I pounced on the loose ball and before the referee could blow for the penalty kick, I had side-footed the ball past Suckling from six yards out.

Despite my recent inactivity, I was in no mood to treat the game lightly and was booked in the first half following one or two telling tackles.

"Alex Ferguson's arrival at Old Trafford had blown away the cobwebs that had gathered during the latter days of Ron Atkinson's reign"

If one or two of the City players felt aggrieved following their cup exit, it was nothing compared to what the Arsenal players felt a fortnight later, during the League leaders 2-0 defeat at Old Trafford. Arsenal, not only lost their unbeaten twenty-two match unbeaten record, but also their concentration and tempers as the match boiled over.

The match was certainly not for the faint hearted, with one player sent off and six booked. I was never one to stand back and let the others take the knocks and tackles and was, as always, in the thick of things. Arsenal did not like this approach and many fingers were pointed in my direction, especially from north London, after the match.

With only twenty minutes gone, a crunching double tackle on Rocastle and Davis saw me booked by referee George Tyson, as the game bubbled away towards the interval, I might have done better with a header from a Gordon Strachan corner which hit the side netting.

After the break, when tempers should have cooled, Rocastle followed team-mate Williams into the referee's note book shortly before Gordon Strachan opened the scoring with a searing drive. Arsenal, were clearly disappointed at going behind and the game boiled over a few minutes later.

On the touch line, in front of the main stand and the dug outs, David Rocastle was once again the victim of one of my tackles and in retaliation kicked out. This left the referee with no option but to send him off, due to his earlier booking. I moved away from the scene, which proved a wise move, as all hell broke loose, with Viv Anderson having to be forcibly

restrained from getting his hands on me. Many felt that I should have accompanied the arsenal player from the pitch. Arsenal, however, had now lost their concentration and we took advantage of the situation and scored a second goal through Terry Gibson.

If the match itself was considered volatile then it was rather feeble compared with the after match furore.

David O'Leary (Arsenal)

"It all started when he tackled me in the first few minutes. I turned and played the ball away and then came the tackle. It was no ordinary tackle. He went in like some sort of fruitcake. In my view, he was out to pole-axe me. He knew what he was doing. He knew he couldn't take me on for pace and he knew he couldn't take the ball. He got me with a knee high tackle that ripped off the back of my sock. You expect the referee to take action, but he didn't. The referee let it go without a word of warning to Whiteside.The tackle summed up Norman Whiteside. And that was the start of the bad feeling in the match. The same player was involved all the time throughout he game and he was getting away with it. He was like a wild nutter throughout the whole match. Don't ask me why he tackled like that. He was going in so late. He was allowed to run around like a lunatic. He seems to get away with it more at Old Trafford. He went over the top on so many people."

Nobby Stiles (former United player)

"Sure, Norman does naughty things and let's be honest, I did too. He's not a saint. But Norman has got to learn. I went into tackles which were 70-30 against me, but I learned not to attempt the impossible."

Alex Ferguson

"Norman may be over enthusiastic, but will learn to curb that. I would be disappointed if nearly all my players were upset by one of their rivals and lost their cool as Arsenal did."

Mike Langley (The Sunday People)

"Arsenal's reaction was a bit rich coming from a club whose greatest season featured Peter Storey of the cold eyes and hell-fire tackle. Yes, the same club that now employs Steve Williams who is inclined to do at the back door what storey did at the front. Norman's put himself about ever since finding out that senior pros were queuing up to test his teenage courage. Now they queue up to get out of his way."

My booking against Arsenal was my eighth of the season and took me over the disciplinary-point mark, leading to a two match suspension. This was in fact my second suspension of the season, having been banned for three matches for reaching twenty-one points in November. At the end of the season, I was suspended for one match and fined £250 for reaching forty-one points when up before the FA Disciplinary Committee.

On this occasion, I was accompanied to Lancaster gate by Bobby Charlton, who assured the FA that I would be better behaved in the future. This wasn't the best of times to be out of the first-team picture as Alex Ferguson had hinted that many of the squad might not be around next season, so everyone was effectively playing for their United careers.

Missing a 0-0 draw at Charlton and a 3-1 home win against Watford, I returned to face Chelsea at Stamford Bridge and went on to play in twelve of the remaining fifteen games, scoring only once, against Coventry City on the penultimate day of a rather disappointing season.

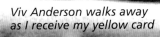

*Viv Anderson walks away
as I receive my yellow card*

Chapter 9

FERGIE'S ARRIVAL
Season 1987-88

During the summer of 1987, Alex Ferguson took time to reflect on his first six months in charge at Old Trafford and slowly began to remould Manchester United into a much more formidable side. Viv Anderson and Brian McClair were signed, while an attempt to bring Kevin Drinkell from Norwich City came to nothing.

It was strange to have Viv in the same team, as we had always found him as a bit of a competitor, always involved in the thick of things when we faced Arsenal. Now I had to be nice to him! As it turned out, he was a really nice bloke and we soon became good friends and remain so to this day, even going as far as becoming business partners.

"The pre-season friendlies gave me plenty of time to readjust to my striking role and I gradually began to enjoy it up front again"

I suppose that the Arsenal of the 1980s were little different to that of today. If everything was going their way then they were happy, but as soon as anyone began to play hard, then they did not like it one bit. I can always remember Robbo coming back from England duty and telling me that Viv Anderson was always at him, trying to get him to admit that I was a dirty player. Robbo of course would have none of it and always told him so. Viv, however, never let up.

When he arrived, I ambled over to say hello, while at the same time mentioning that I had heard that he considered me this and that. Poor Viv did not know what to say, but once my face broke into a smile, he knew I was simply having him on.

Strangely, following Viv's arrival, as with Brian McClair and Jesper Olsen, Alex Ferguson, for some completely unknown reason asked me to show them around Manchester and make sure that they settled in ok. Why he picked me, I have no idea, but I suppose he knew that I knew all the best pubs and hotels, so they couldn't really go wrong on that account. I'm still surprised that he trusted me!

Before the season got underway, the manager took me aside and told me that he was going to play me up front alongside Brian McClair as he felt this was his best option. The boss accepted that I preferred midfield, but thought that both the club and myself would benefit from his decision. I also knew there were some doubts regarding my pace, or lack of it to be more precise, but many had overcome that. Kenny Dalglish with Liverpool was a perfect example.

The pre-season friendlies gave me plenty of time to readjust to my striking role and against IS Halmia of Sweden, I grabbed four goals in our 9-1 win. I gradually began to enjoy it up front again and began to form an understanding with Brian McClair.

My pre-season build up went even better than I could have hoped for, with selection for the Football League side to face the Rest of the World at Wembley in the Mercantile Credit Centenary Classic. Augmented with the likes of Maradona, Alberto and Platini, the Rest of the World were beaten 3-0 which was mainly thanks to the Manchester United contingent in the Football League ranks.

As well as myself, Bryan Robson, inspired us in midfield, scoring a couple of the goals, while Paul McGrath kept Maradona well under control. Although only named as substitute, I came off the bench to score the second goal, following good work by Liam Brady.

Bryan Robson

"Norman is my best pal at United, but that has nothing to do with my feelings that he could develop into as great a player as Kenny Dalglish, doing the same sort of job.

There are plenty of similarities, they both shield the ball and hold up the play superbly. They can both score clever goals and neither man allows himself to be intimidated or knocked about.

He thoroughly enjoys putting himself around, but I have never seen him deliberately hurt anybody. He's not a dirty player. Hard yes, but not sly like some players. Not an over the top merchant. He's robust and tough and such a big lad his physical presence gives him a look that is too often mis-interpreted as dirty.

All his faults are youthful vigour, a competitive edge that sometimes pushes him to flash point. But then nobody regrets it more than he does. We talk about it a lot when we're having a pint or two. And I've told him he has got to cool his rashness. He really is a brilliant footballer, the best in Britain, with the best finishing touch in the game."

I took it as a big honour to grace the same pitch as the likes of Maradona and Platini, even though I had already faced them both in European competitions with United. Michel Platini in particular was very difficult to play against and I am very grateful that I did not have to face him in direct opposition. Any player who was voted the European Footballer of the Year on three separate occasions was obviously something special.

All the game's honours seemed to come his way, as if he was a magnet, winning the European Cup with Juventus in 1985, scoring the only goal in that infamous match against Liverpool in the Heysel Stadium in Brussels. A year earlier, he had captained France to the European Championship, scoring nine of his country's fifteen goals.

He had actually retired as Juventus captain in the summer prior to that Rest of the World match at Wembley, but even without proper training and at the age of thirty-two, he was magical, with every move seemingly going through him. He was upstaged on this occasion though as Bryan Robson snatched the man of the match award.

Another overseas player I found a tough opponent was German defender Karl-Heinz Forster, a no-nonsense stopper, who played in two World Cup Finals and a European Championship Final for his country.

"It was a big honour to grace the same pitch as the likes of Maradona and Platini"

On the home front though, it was the Liverpool duo of Alan Hansen and Mark Lawrenson who always provided a testing afternoon, ensuring that you had always to be at your best when facing them. They weren't just excellent in their defensive play, they were also more than capable of playing with the ball at their feet, something that many defenders found uncomfortable.

Much of Liverpool's success was due to Hansen and Lawrenson and I think at times they did not receive all the credit they were due. Thankfully we only had to face them twice a season.

The close season had also seen me launch the 'Norman Whiteside Fan Club', from an office in Altrincham, something that few (if any) other players of that time could boast. Members were charged £7.95 and for their outlay they received a membership card, T-shirt, signed photograph, colour poster, fact file and a quarterly newsletter in which I kept them up to date with (most) of my on and off-field activities.

Our 1987-88 League campaign began at the Dell and the Whiteside machine continued to roll. Goals in the 25th and 32nd minute, the first a shot through a crowded goalmouth, the second a header at the far post. A Danny Wallace double however took the shine of both mine and the team's performance and earned the Saints a point.

Arsenal, at Old Trafford, was played out with bated breath following last season's confrontation, but it passed without a whimper. But I sprang back into the spotlight against Watford three days later.

John Richardson (The Sun)
"But unless Whiteside's naked aggression can be curbed, it threatens to dent United's title tilt.
Backheeling Gibbs in the face after losing out in a tackle happened so soon after half time, that I wasn't even back in my seat. But from what I have heard about it, if Whiteside had been a Watford player, he would have been hung, drawn and quartered."

The Sun seemed to dwell rather much on the incident, but I think the fact that some of the other newspapers didn't even give it a mention signifies that they were making something out of nothing.

"Suddenly, the club pulled out - was it the beginning of the end of a love affair?"

After appearing in the opening twelve fixtures of the season, I failed to put together a decent run during the remainder of the season, with six together, not including substitute outings, the best that I could manage. Although I did fit in the odd appearance with Northern Ireland.

Following something of a promising start in the League, we failed to pick up points against teams that we should have beaten, like Charlton and Southampton at home as the season progressed. We also lost 2-0 to Oxford United in the Littlewoods Cup. It was a challenging period at United, as many of us were more or less on trial and if we did not perform then we knew that the manager would have no hesitation in moving us on.

We sprang back, beating Arsenal at Highbury, but losing there in the FA Cup. I took my goals total to ten when I scored at the Baseball Ground, while the win against Derby and those against Coventry and Chelsea kept us handily placed to maintain a challenge at the top end of the table.

In early March, the manager made a move for Danish international Michael Laudrup, who was at that time playing for Juventus and it was suggested that I was to be used in a part exchange deal. The deal, however, failed to materialise, with Laudrup eventually moving to Glasgow Rangers. Shortly after the revelations of the proposed transfer though, my future at United came into serious doubt, when the promised new contract that would have kept me at the club until the 1990s failed to materialise.

To be honest, I did not know where I stood, as it was very important that I got some re-assuring answers to my long-term future. It had always been my idea to stay at United as long as possible, maybe until the end of my career. Negotiations had been started and were in fact going well. An extension to my current deal had been agreed and we were really very close to settling to everything in principle.

A photocall at Old Trafford

Suddenly, out of the blue, the club pulled out and I was never given a satisfactory reason why. My whole future was now in question and I was unsettled for the first time in my career. Was it the beginning of the end of a love affair?

Speculation at the time was rife that it was Alex Ferguson who brought an end to the talks between myself and Martin Edwards, telling the chairman that if I wanted a new deal then I had to go out and prove that I deserved it.
This was a stance that the manager was to reverse in the years ahead, making it a priority that most, if not all, his players were tied up on long-term contracts.

Although rather saddened by the outcome, I did not storm off, demanding a transfer or a showdown, but the news did create interest from other clubs and I am sure a few more seats would have been filled for my return to competitive football against Grimsby Town, following an injury, if the game had not been postponed.

A link to Graeme Souness at Glasgow Rangers was nothing more than newspaper talk, but the name of Norman Whiteside was pencilled into numerous notebooks and a close eye would be kept by many clubs on the situation between myself and United.

It was around this time that the rumours began to circulate that Paul McGrath and myself spent more time with pint glasses in our hands than footballs at our feet, with former United star Pat Crerand's pub in Altrincham a favoured rendezvous. Paddy would always deny that either of us were ever the worst of drink. News of reputed adventures of course reached the ears of Alex Ferguson, who kept a close eye on the situation.

By the end of March, things had came to a head, mainly due to the stalling of my new contract and I made the club and the supporters aware that I intended leaving at the end of the season. I felt that my career had gone stale and come to a halt. A new challenge was what I felt was needed, something to rekindle my ambitions. A move abroad would also have been acceptable, as the opportunities had been there before and pushed to the side. I felt then that I was perhaps too young to take such a big step, but things were different now.

The decision was not a spur of the moment thing and was something that I had thought a lot about for quite some time. I had also found it difficult to get wound up for some of the games, with the cup ties in particular failing to produce a buzz. So much had unsettled me around this time, but the collapse of the contract talks left me very disappointed. I also felt disappointed for the supporters that I was unable to bring them the League Championship that they craved for so much.

My decision seemed to catch the club unawares and no immediate announcement regarding my future was made, with the only comment being that the matter would be discussed at a board meeting the following week.

Alex Ferguson
"Norman's request did not come as a surprise. It is not normal though for United players to ask to leave the club. I still value him, both as a player and a person. I've no argument whatsoever with Norman.
He is under treatment for an Achilles injury at the moment, so the decision on his selection for the first team has been done for me."

I was uncertain as to the manager's thoughts on the situation and wondered if I would be considered for the first team in the weeks ahead. The question was answered prior to the match against Liverpool at Anfield on Easter Monday, when I was named as substitute. With only half-a-dozen games left to play, there was not much of an opportunity for me to prove my fitness to prospective buyers should my transfer request be granted, but I think everyone knew what I was capable off.

This was certainly the case at Anfield, as I came off the bench to give the travelling United support what could have been a lasting memory. It also proved to any interested parties that I still possessed fire and determination and could do a good job for them in midfield.

Despite taking an early lead through Bryan Robson after only three minutes, we found ourselves 3-1 down two minutes after half time. To make matters worse, Colin Gibson was sent off eleven minutes later, leaving us a real uphill struggle.

About four minutes before this set back, Alex Ferguson must have considered his options and decided that he had nothing to lose. Perhaps on the other hand he knew that if anyone could give the ten men some inspiration and perhaps salvage something out of the game then it was the 'want-away' man. If this was to be my swan song, then I was going to go out on a high. As I warmed up along the touch line, it was like being thrown to the lions in the Coliseum, with all the crowd's venom hurled in my direction.

The first Liverpool player to come my way was John Barnes, who caught the force of my elbow. Missed by the referee but no-one else. Soon afterwards, I bulldozed Steve McMahon and to appease the baying Merseyside hoards, the referee booked me. Liverpool were now well aware that if they were wanting to keep their lead then they were going to have to compete for it.

Although just called into the fray, I took the game by the scuff of the neck and slowly we began to sense that we indeed have a chance of salvaging something from the afternoon. Bryan Robson reduced the arrears, scoring his second, in the 66th minute and as a crescendo of boos echoed around Anfield every time I touched the ball, I pushed the ball through to Gordon Strachan eleven minutes later to score the equaliser.

"If this was to be my swan song, then I was going to go out on a high"

Barney Chilton (Editor of the Red News Fanzine)
"The incident between Norman and McMahon is one of those memorable United moments. It is up there with the best of them and is still talked about today by those who were there."

Following the dramatic ninety minutes in the hate-filled Anfield arena, I caused an even bigger controversy around Liverpool a couple of days later, when I was quoted in the press as saying that Liverpool considered themselves bigger than anybody and when someone like me stands up to them, then they do not like it and can't take it. The Kop didn't like my competitive style and the challenge on McMahon wasn't even a hard one. At worst, I might have stood on his little toe, but there was never any intent to do him any damage. I did admit to catching John Barnes with my elbow, but that was the only bad challenge that I made.

The funniest thing about the Anfield clash was after the game when I was sitting alone thinking back over our fight back to draw 3-3, when a couple of policemen came over and asked if I wanted an escort back to the team coach. I simply laughed and told them that they must be joking.

The board meeting upon which my future hinged was held on April 5th and the outcome was as expected, but unwanted. I could go.

Alex Ferguson
"Norman was upset when I refused him a new five-year contract while he still had two years to run on his current one. It is a point of principle, not something just aimed at Norman. Other players have been disappointed with similar approaches. In Norman's case perhaps his pride was hurt. Anyway, he asked for a transfer and really there is no point having players whose heart is not playing for you.

"I think there will be interest in him because it is hard to get good players. If he is not sold then he will stay at old Trafford and play on. At the end of the day that might be a good thing for United. If a player does it on the field then you want him to stay. I rate Norman very highly and replacing him will not be easy. He is a marvellous player. He's done it all and he is still only a kid."

"There was no turning back - I had lost faith in the club "

My fleeting appearance at Anfield, while saluted by the United support, came in for much criticism from the Liverpool factions. It was not just the fanatical supporters who had bayed their dislike towards me from the terracing, but former Kop favourite Tommy Smith, himself not adverse to playing the game hard, spoke out against my tactics.

Tommy Smith (former Liverpool player)
"This fella puts Norman Hunter and myself to shame. He thinks he's a hard man yet he doesn't tackle properly. He's so late so often in the tackle that he's an embarrassment. The only answer is to send him off the instant it happens and repeat the dosage until he learns his lesson.

He could have broken Steve's leg. He should have gone straight down the tunnel. He wouldn't have lasted ten minutes in the sixties and seventies. He would have been sent off regularly. It seems to me that talking back at referee's has become a worse offence than dangerous tackles. Whiteside isn't even cute with his tackling. How would he have fared against Bobby Collins, Johnny Giles and Jimmy Morrissey. He's so late that I've wondered how he's managed to catch the train on United away trips."

Any thoughts I had of securing an early move to pastures new were hit on the head when the club announced that I would have to stay until the end of the season. It was disappointing, but as I was under contract there was really nothing that I could do.

The United supporters, with whom I had always enjoyed a passionate relationship, caused me a sleepless night before my first outing at Old Trafford after announcing my intentions to leave. I didn't know what to expect against Luton Town, but I thought, and was hoping, that the fans would understand how I felt and why I had made the decision. Unfortunately, when my name was announced as one of the substitutes there was something of a sour response. Perhaps it is just as well that I did not get on that afternoon.

My team-mate and off-the-field buddy Paul McGrath had also shocked the club and supporters by also asking for a transfer soon after I had and his arrival onto the pitch against Luton was greeted with boos and calls of traitor. Neither lasted too long though.

My first Official Man Utd Jacket

Most of the early interest in me was purely newspaper talk and there were no approaches to the club until around the end of April. Then, it was not from Italy as many expected, but from Greek side Olympiakos. The manager called me into his office and said that they had been in touch and asked if I would be interested in joining them.

Whilst not one of the biggest club's in the world, a move there did sound quite attractive, so I said that I would be interested. We then sat back and waited for them to come back with something more definite a few days later.

Within a week, my name was emblazoned over the back page of the Daily Mirror, with a headline that would cause many to choke on their cornflakes. There was no mention of a move to Greece. Instead, above my name, in large black letters, was the headline, 'I Want To Play For Liverpool.'

It was a little tongue in cheek, but yes, I would have went. In fact, I would have went anywhere at that time as things were so bad at United. There was no turning back and I had lost faith in the club after they had turned down what I considered a reasonable request. I thought that I would be a United player for life and I honestly never thought that it would come to this.

I also thought that the £1.5 million price tag that Alex Ferguson put on my head was ridiculous. I was never worth a million never mind more than that. There were certainly few teams about who could afford such a figure.

Jim McGregor, puts me back together

Chapter 10

INJURY SETBACKS
Season 1988-89

Early July brought new developments and it began to look even more likely that I would be moving abroad, with the prospect of a move to Greece now stronger than ever, as both Olympiakos and Panathinaikos were prepared to offer in the region of £2 million.

In an effort to be fully fit for the coming season, no matter who I would be playing with, I returned to United's Cliff training ground before the other players in an effort to lift my fitness to a level that would be acceptable to everyone. Unfortunately, it did not have the desired effect, as an Achilles tendon injury, picked up in training, ruled me out of United's pre-season tour of Sweden, as I had to have the ankle in plaster for ten days.

Upon resuming training, I was eased back towards first-team action with a place in a United eleven that travelled up to the north-east to play a friendly against Fourth Division Hartlepool. Also included in the squad were the likes of Viv Anderson, Paul McGrath and Mike Duxbury but their presence made little difference to the outcome of the match, with the home side recording a sensational 6-0 victory. Thankfully I was spared some of the embarrassment in the humiliation, by being taken off at half time due to a recurrence of my Achilles injury.

The set back was a big blow, not only to myself but also to the manager, as we had quite a few injuries at this time and we certainly did not want to be left behind in the early days of the new season. Despite the friction between us, there was still a possibility of reconciliation, brought about by the fact that there had been no more interest in me and also because of the retirement of Remi Moses due to injury. This had created a midfield vacancy alongside Bryan Robson and if I could regain my fitness, then you could never tell what might happen.

Many of the supporters would obviously have to be won over again after I had stated that I had lost the enthusiasm I once had for the club and my urge to get away.

My fitness, however, was the main problem and as my team mates got back into league action against Queens Park Rangers at Old Trafford, I was on the comeback trail again, this time against Swindon Town. Frustratingly, once more I failed to last the ninety minutes, limping off with my Achilles once again causing a problem.

A visit to the club specialist did not bring good news, as he told me that I would require an immediate operation, with a further two or three months on the sidelines.

"Supporters would have to be won over again after I had stated that I had lost enthusiasm for the club"

Alex Ferguson
"The first thing that Norman has got to do is get back to playing again at the top level. Then he can do something about his career. When he is back in the United team, we can discuss things. At the moment it's stalemate and nobody knows what the future holds. We were all hoping that he would come back from the summer ready to accept the challenge because that's the kind of player he is. When he is fired up, quite a few people in the game really worry about him. But everything has been in mid-air because of this injury."

The last thing I wanted was to be out of the first-team picture, but it did give me some time to get away from the pressure that had built up over the past few weeks regarding the transfer business and it also gave me more time to reassess the position. Getting back to fitness was now my number one priority and after all, I was only twenty-three with a good few years left in me yet. Hopefully, the black cloud that had overshadowed my career of late would soon disperse.

In early October, as I began easing my way back once again, the manager hinted that there was indeed a place in the Manchester United side for me. He also admitted that if I could contribute to an improvement on the previous season, then he would be more than happy to sit down and discuss the future with me.

My plans for returning to action in October following the operation hit a stumbling block, as I felt a reaction during a training session and I had to have the ankle put back in plaster. It was now going to be nearer to Christmas before I would be ready for first-team duties again.

Results in the opening weeks of the season had certainly not been flattering and United failed to score in the opening two games, but they then recorded three straight wins without conceding a goal. However, a run of seven draws and one defeat in the following eight games showed that there was clearly something lacking in the squad and as I frustratedly watched my team-mates struggle along I felt that if I was able to play then I would have been able to turn some of those draws into victories.

The plaster came off in early November and following a week doing little more than walking, the surgeon allowed me to do some remedial work in the gym. Being out was absolute murder, a nightmare. But, the club stuck by me despite the recent friction and I was determined to repay them once I got back into action.

Alex Ferguson
"Certainly there will be no problem as far as I am concerned. He is welcome to pick up his career at Old Trafford. The things he said last season can be forgotten. It is up to him of course. He hasn't played for six months, which is a long time in football and we all want to see him back. The quicker he is playing again the better it will be for both him and the club. We could certainly do with him playing again."

It wasn't long before I made the headlines again with an appearance at Old Trafford, but it was a reasonable throw in from the pitch that the action took place. As I was not included in the match action, I found my way into the Sharp Sponsors Lounge, where I enjoyed a glass of champagne. The manager, of course, had eyes and ears everywhere, not just around the ground but all over the Manchester postcode and I soon found myself in hot water.

It was in the club rules that players were not permitted to drink in the sponsor's suite and despite my non-involvement in the game I was pulled up for my misconduct and fined two weeks wages, which was around £3,000.

As November drew to a close, I began to worry as to what my future held. I was disappointed that I had started only one League game since February 23rd, but was completely shattered, when I was told that my Achilles had not responded as hoped following surgery and I was now booked in for a visit to a top London specialist for a second opinion. Worried I certainly was.

Throughout most of this time, I had Paul McGrath for company, as he was also suffering from long spells on the sidelines with knee injuries. As 1988 turned into 1989 Paul eased his way back into the first team and made a telling come back against Liverpool, coming on as substitute in our 3-1 win at Old Trafford on New Year's Day. He played against

Middlesbrough twenty four hours later, but suddenly withdrew from the team to play Queens Park Rangers in the FA Cup on January 7th, telling Alex Ferguson that he had a problem with his knee.

But as the crowds descended upon Old Trafford for the all-important cup-tie, the rumour machines were being cranked up to breaking point.

The manager had been told that Manchester United's answer to the Lone Ranger and Tonto had been out on the town late at night and that they had both appeared on Granada Television's "Kick-Off" Friday night programme the worse for wear. Some who watched the programme said that it was impossible to tell, but Paul later admitted that perhaps he did have one or two too many. Me? I had no game to worry about the following day.

In any case, we were both summoned to Old Trafford, where with PFA chief Gordon Taylor present, we faced Alex Ferguson and Martin Edwards. Our futures were very much on the line as we had both had written and verbal warnings in the past.

My situation was perhaps not quite as serious as that of Paul's, as I was unavailable for selection. The manager also felt that I still had something to contribute to the club and had a career that was worth saving. So, deciding to go for broke, they sent me to the Lilleshall Sports Rehabilitation Centre on a month's get fit programme.

This course of action had a double effect. Firstly, it gave me the opportunity to work on my injured ankle, receiving first class care in reassessing my overall fitness. Secondly and more importantly from the club's point of view, it kept me away from Paul McGrath, the main source of United's disapproval, who was considered to be a bad and disruptive influence.

The friendship between Paul and myself was cemented way back in the days when we both lived with Mr and Mrs Fannon and along with Bryan Robson, we could have been Manchester's Three Musketeers. It was mainly Paul and I who were together and apparently in trouble. Robbo could go out drinking at night, wake up in the morning, go training and never be up nor down. Paul on the other hand always seemed to be a bit worse for wear than me.

Paul was a brilliant footballer, similar in style to Liverpool's Hansen and Lawrenson, but a much better player. Like me, he suffered more than his fair share of injuries and we would spend a lot of time together in the treatment room. Who knows what might have been if we had both steered clear of injuries. He would have certainly been one of the best central defenders in the world.

"Summoned to Old Trafford, our futures were very much on the line"

As for Robbo, he was undoubtedly the best player that I ever shared a football pitch with and we soon became friends following his move from West Bromwich Albion. I wasn't too sure about being seen out with him when he had the permed hair, but he eventually got rid of that! He was also a regular companion in the treatment room and I think that we all went out for a few pints to forget the misfortunes we suffered with injuries.

RESIDENCE
5, OLD HALL ROAD,
BROUGHTON PARK,
SALFORD,
M7 0JJ.
TEL. 061-740 1201.

MR. ALAN GLASS

20, ST JOHN STREET,
MANCHESTER.
M3 4FA.

TEL: 061-834 1010

AG/MJ

26th July 1979.

Dear Dr. McHugh,

re: Norman Whiteside
_____

I saw this young man. He is well built and complains of pain in both groins.

When I saw him, I found quite remarkable loss of medial rotation in both hips especially on the left side and suspected that he might have a slipped upper femoral epiphysis. Fortunately, my clinical guess was not backed up radiologically and in fact the x-rays show no bony lesion.

I think that he requires graduated exercises and some short wave diathermy. It is difficult to determine the future in this case in the long term but certainly he could be encouraged to continue with the professional football career even on a medium term basis.

Kind regards,

Yours sincerely,

Dr. F. McHugh,
c/o Manchester United F.C.,
Old Trafford,
MANCHESTER 16.

Like his nickname, Robbo was indeed 'Captain Fantastic' and he often won us games on his own. It was a big loss when he was not in the side. If I ever had to pick my all-star eleven, then not only would Bryan be the first name that I would put down, he would also be my captain. I am sure that he would run through a brick wall if you asked him to and it was for the benefit of the team. A top man.

My period in 'solitary confinement' at Lilleshall was something of a real eye opener excusing the pun, it had something of a sobering effect on me. I had to sleep on a sort of camp bed in a dormitory, which in itself was completely alien, as I had always been used to the best of hotels with United and Northern Ireland. That alone, brought me back down to earth with a bump.

Upon my return to the more familiar and luxurious surroundings of Old Trafford, I resumed light training. Progress was made and with spring in the air, as I slowly got back into some sort of shape, I was included in the United reserve side to face Everton at Goodison Park on March 4th. Despite my long-term omission from football of any kind, I was soon involved in the action. A tackle here and there, a couple of runs, with one of my passes making the first goal in our 2-2 draw. There were one or two glimpses of the old skills for the sparse crowd scattered around the ground and it was pleasing just to be involved again with United.

Coming through my initial return to football action, I was earmarked to face Newcastle United's second string at Old Trafford, allowing United's die hard supporters who followed not only the first team but also the reserves, the opportunity of welcoming me back to the fold.

My second game back, this time captaining the side, also resulted in a draw, but this was of little significance to the United management, as, more importantly, I once again came through ninety minutes of football unscathed. I was, to say the least, well satisfied with my progress.

Alex Ferguson

"Norman certainly wants to play again and we saw his determination last night.
He played most of the match with a temperature of 103 and did well to stay on. We would have had him off at half time but we had a further two players who were injured and required substituting.
Norman wasn't at all well and obviously was going down with 'flu. It says a lot for his commitment on his comeback that he carried on."

The day after that second comeback match, I announce that I was ready to pledge my future to Manchester United. I had never really wanted to leave and only wanted an extension on my contract so that I could be with them for the rest of my career. That upset me a bit. Then everything fell on top of me with the injury and the other things. It was all very frustrating, as I am not a great watcher of matches.

Fortunately, the injury was now behind me and I was happy with the way things were going. There was an FA Cup tie on the immediate horizon, but I was more than happy just to take one game at a time.

I still had another year on my contract to go, and in those twelve months, I was going to go out and prove that I was worth further extensiont. I still had to prove my fitness, but I had cleared one of the hurdles on the course by once again getting on good terms with Alex Ferguson and the problems of a year ago were certainly behind me now.

The high temperature that almost curtailed my reserve-team outing against Newcastle United turned out to be chickenpox, which obviously forced me out of any planned comeback against Aston Villa or a third reserve-team outing against Liverpool.

I still had my eyes firmly fixed on taking some sort of part against Nottingham Forest in the sixth round of the FA Cup and my name, missing from the sports pages for so long suddenly sprang to the fore in the days leading up to the important cup tie.

Forest manager Brian Clough, never one to shy away from the headlines, stoked up the pre-match interest by claiming that if Alex Ferguson, who had apparently declared an interest in Forest's Neil Webb, wanted his midfielder then Norman Whiteside would have to be part of any deal agreed. As it was, I failed to make the Forest match, United lost 1-0 and the Webb – Whiteside transfer talk evaporated into thin air.

> "I felt in really good shape and ready to make the step up
> to first team level - I was now biting at the bit
> and couldn't wait to get back"

A further strength and confidence building second string appearance was to follow at Rochdale's Spotland ground. Again I came through the ninety minutes without any problems during our 3-1 win. I was certainly pleased with my performance and felt that my long awaited return to first-team football was just around the corner. Following our cup defeat against Forest, Alex Ferguson had to rally his disappointed troops and as our results of late were something of a mixed bag, I kept my fingers crossed that I would manage a few appearances in the dozen League fixtures that remained of season 1988-89.

I was certainly building up my match fitness, as yet another reserve match, this time against Blackburn Rovers, was followed by a friendly in the totally unfamiliar surroundings of the Isle of Man, a match that celebrated the Manx FA Centenary. I didn't see any of those cat's without any tails during my brief trip to the Isle of Man, but I did score my first goal since returning to match action in United's 6-0 win.

With a fifth comeback match under my belt, I felt in really good shape and I was certainly ready to make the step up to first-team level if and when required. I was now biting at the bit and couldn't wait to get back.

As I was enjoying a rather leisurely afternoon in the Isle of Man, Nottingham Forest repeated their 1-0 FA Cup success over United with a 2-0 defeat at the City Ground on Easter Monday. A result that ended any hopes that we had of finishing in the top three or four positions in the League. However, I still had a lot to play for.

My return to fitness had obviously come too late to rescue United's season, but my re-emergence into the first-team picture was looked forward to by the sometimes fickle United supporter's, who had now almost forgotten about the transfer request and other minor events.

Viv Anderson was another player who had been out for some time and the manager stated that if he could get us both back, then he could begin to look to the future, continuing to play the likes of Russell Beardsmore and giving opportunities to up and coming youngsters such as Giuliano Maiorana.

My prolonged injury had not only caused Alex Ferguson problems, but Billy Bingham was also forced to struggle along, perhaps a bit more so, as Northern Ireland did not have too many players to call upon. Billy, to his credit had kept in close

contact throughout my spell on the sidelines, something that I was always grateful for and assured me that I was in his World Cup qualifying plans.

Another reserve-team outing, against Huddersfield Town, again finding the back of the net, confirmed that I was ready for first-team action. With mainly youngsters around me, I was able to orchestrate the game from midfield, but as full time approached, the telling moment of my recovery occurred.

The ball, bobbling around in the middle of the pitch, suddenly broke between myself and a more youthful opponent and making a split second decision I threw myself into a crunching tackle, coming clear with the ball and leaving the lad sprawled on the ground. The smiles on the United bench clearly signified that Norman Whiteside was indeed back.

With an Arsenal visit to Old Trafford beckoning, I, like the United supporter's was looking forward to a thrilling confrontation. It had been 379 days since my name had last appeared in the Manchester United first team starting line up, but in the end, it was down to the manager whether or not I was to add a few more days on to that total.

It had certainly been a bad year, but it was at an end now and my return to full fitness could not have come at a better time, as twenty-four hours prior to the Arsenal match, Bryan Robson pulled up in training with a hamstring injury, casting indoubt his inclusion in the line up.

As it turned out, both Robbo and I made the starting line-up and as the game got under way, I treated the familiar Old Trafford stage with some trepidation, but the old confidence soon returned.

Patrick Barclay (Independent)
"Norman Whiteside, on his first appearance for a year, used the ball remarkably well in the cloying conditions, though some of his tackles were so late that the intended victim had gone."

In the opening exchanges, I felt a little lost and perhaps a little out of my depth, on the muddy rain-sodden pitch, but as the game went on the slow moving ball helped me pace myself better through the ninety minutes. Although I must say that I was quite tired at the end.

My United return immediately prompted Billy Bingham to recall me into his Northern Ireland plans and I found myself in the under-23 line-up, as captain, against the Republic of Ireland in Dublin. It was nice to be back and allowed me the chance of building on the ninety minutes I had against Arsenal.

Billy Bingham (Northern Ireland manager)
"I watched him against Arsenal and thought he did extremely well in the circumstances. The main thing is that Alex Ferguson gave him the full ninety minutes. Alex was delighted with the prospect of this under-23 international because he wants Norman to get as many games under his belt as possible. From my point of view, he will be an asset to the under-23's. Although he has been around a long time, Norman is still in his early twenties and his experience will be of benefit to the rest of the squad."

My return to the international scene as an unde-age player did not bring much in the way of enjoyment, as the Republic youngsters recorded a 3-0 victory. Adding to my disappointment, I received a slight groin injury which forced me to miss the match against Derby County at Old Trafford.

After a period of prolonged darkness, when looking at my future through the bottom of a glass, which at times seemed anything but bright, everything now seemed to be on track and heading in the right direction. I had played and completed a number of games, but perhaps more importantly, all talks of a move away from Manchester United were now forgotten.

Alex Ferguson
"He's going nowhere. His career is at stake and nothing matters except that he should get back to the form that swept him to the top. Everything else is unimportant. We can forget the speculation about transfers or whether Norman still wants to leave. He isn't on the list. He never was. All we said was that we would listen to offers because he said he wanted to go. I don't expect him to come back and eat humble pie because he has had a year out of the game since then with his Achilles injury. It's in the interests of the club and the player that he regains his old form."

"A defeat at Southampton compounded another afternoon of despair and although there were another three games to play, it was to be my last game of the season"

Surprisingly, when the initial transfer talk surfaced, there was practically no interest, but now that I was re-emerging onto the scene and with the transfer deadline approaching, the speculation was again beginning to surface. West Ham United had reportedly had a bid turned down and Everton were also considering making an offer.

Injury and suspension to Clayton Blackmore and Bryan Robson thrust me back into first-team action as United struggled to salvage something from their season. Returning against Charlton Athletic, which ended in another defeat for United, I suffered a recurrence of the groin strain, delaying my return to the full Northern Ireland side. I was, however, able to play for United the following Saturday against Coventry.

A crowd of only 27,799 watch a lacklustre United performance, our third consecutive defeat and our fourth match without scoring, resulting in the disappointed crowd booing us from the pitch at both half time and full time. No one escaped their wrath.

David Keenan (The Daily Telegraph)
"Hundreds of fans left well before the end of a match United never looked capable of winning. They had seen Robson, as so often this season, shoulder the burden of an otherwise lethargic midfield in which Whiteside played at half pace."

Results continued to go against United and even the reserve team, which had been supplemented of late by my presence struggled along and faced relegation to the Central League Division Two at one point.

A 2-1 defeat at Southampton compounded another afternoon of despair for what the press had christened 'Fergie's Flops' and although there were still another three games to play, it was to be my last game of the season, as I suffered a hamstring injury during a very forgettable ninety-minutes.

With the season drawing to a close, with me out of competitive action, transfer speculation again reared its head, when it was reported that I was about to join Glasgow Rangers. Having travelled to Glasgow to watch them in the Scottish Cup Final against local rivals Celtic, someone put two and two together and got five. Having been linked with the Ibrox side on previous occasions I suppose added some fuel to the rumours that talks were taking place regarding an imminent move.

As the memories of a disastrous season began to fade during the summer, everyone began to hope for a vast improvement during the new campaign, as the momentum to this began to build up. If United were going to improve and progress under Alex Ferguson, then it was obvious that reinforcements were required to boost the squad, which at times was far from strong enough.

"After months of despair, it finally looked as though my footballing career had turned the corner"

Any squad improvements almost certainly required additional funds and one asset, which could certainly be cashed in if necessary, was yours truly. Interest was once again reported in prising me away from United, with Spanish side Osasuna and French clubs Monaco and Paris St Germain supposedly those interested. The £1 million transfer fee was, however, a stumbling block for those clubs.

After months of despair and much uncertainty, it finally looked as though my footballing career had turned the corner. A career that a decade earlier had promised so much. After finishing the previous campaign on something of a high, I was looking forward to a short rest before beginning pre-season training in earnest.

It's not my round Robbo!!

MANCHESTER UNITED
v. EVERTON
Sunday 3rd May 1992   **Kick-off 3.00 pm**

SHARP

WHITESIDE

TESTIMON

Official Programme £1

Chapter 11

FAREWELL UNITED

Season 1989-90

Many players almost despise the summer slog as the muscles and body in general, gets retuned to the physical exertion. But for once, I was itching to jump in the car and head for The Cliff training ground, desperate to be back playing in the First Division on a regular basis, following so long on the sidelines.

With the first week of July barely stroked off the calendar, Osasuna were on the telephone to Old Trafford, tabling a surprise £500,000 bid. The Spanish First Division side apparently wanted me to replace former Liverpool player Michael Robinson, who had been forced to quit the game through injury. The one-time Republic of Ireland player was actually acting as a go-between on the proposed transfer.

The initial offer of £500,000 was rejected by the United board, but it was expected that the Spaniards would be back with a higher offer and that their first one was simply testing the water.

In the meantime, Alex Ferguson had signed Neil Webb and Mike Phelan to bolster the depleted United midfield, so my position was already under threat without a ball even being kicked. It also emphasised to me that if I did get into the team and there was to be any injury problems, then there were certainly no guarantee's that I would immediately reclaim my place.

My position at United was not exactly clear cut in any case. I had heard that chairman Martin Edwards had decided to sell me in an effort to balance the books, with £1 million in the bank much better than an injured player or a highly sellable player on the sidelines. It was also reported that I had my eyes set on a move to Spain and that I had been studying Spanish for the past six months. The latter was certainly untrue. Nearer to home, my former manager, Ron Atkinson now at the helm of Sheffield Wednesday, was widely tipped as being prepared to match the Spaniards £500,000 offer and attempt to prise me over the Pennines.

With doubts relating to my fitness all that was apparently preventing a number of clubs from joining the bidding, Big Ron did indeed admit his interest, but was quick to point out that any transfer would have to be linked to a 'games played' deal.

As the pre-season build up gathered momentum and the transfer market began to bubble, Manchester United were ordered to pay Nottingham Forest £1.5 million for recent acquisition Neil Webb, £600,000 more than they had originally offered. This decision put pressure on Alex Ferguson to off-load one or two players in an effort to reduce the wage bill and recoup some of the outlay. Even more so, if the boss was going to pursue his interest in West Ham's Paul Ince.

> "If I did get into the team and there was injury problems,
> there was no guarantee that I would immediately
> reclaim my place"

£400,000 was quickly replaced in the Manchester United bank account with the sale of my good friend Paul McGrath to Aston Villa and as the ink was drying on this particular deal a new approach was made for my signature. This time it was from a club who had not shown any real previous interest and a club who were prepared to pay the £1million asking price. The club was Everton and Alex Ferguson told me that if I wanted to, I was free to talk to their manager, Colin Harvey, about a move.

Here I am playing for Everton

Colin Harvey
"I was very impressed with Norman's attitude. I know he missed a lot of games last season, but the break may have done him good. After all, he has been a senior player from the age of sixteen. He has promised to give me an answer in the morning."

So, I went home to consider Everton's approach. A move that had just as many pros as it did cons.

I was not guaranteed a regular first-team place at United even when fit, that was clear and certainly had more of a chance in doing so at Goodison Park. There would be no big upheaval in having to move house, as I could remain in my south Manchester home, only having to endure a slightly longer drive to training each day.

But did I really want to leave Manchester United, a club that I had been with since the age of twelve? Here I could enjoy the challenge of fighting for my place. Despite the recent turmoil, I still had feelings for the club. It would be a restless night. Awakening the following morning, I had made up my mind. I was going to cut my ties and sign for Everton.

A fee of £600,000 was agreed between the two clubs, with a further £150,000 added to this when I had played fifty games for the Toffees. Both teams were eager to get the deal tied up, but if there were any last minute delays, then the transfer could be finalised in Tokyo, as both teams were due to meet in a friendly at the Kobe Stadium a week later.

Following my heart-on-the-sleeve performances against the red half of Merseyside, I was obviously going to be even more despised having now joined Everton. This, however, was of little concern to me.

I was now looking forward to the coming season, as I felt that Everton were a big club and certainly ambitious. Hopes of at last winning a Championship medal were strong, as this was my unfulfilled ambition. Firstly though, I had to get back to the standards that I had set myself earlier in my career.

Ron Atkinson
"Everton won't regret signing Norman. He will be a winner for them. And the fee? At £750,000 he's a bargain.
A problem player? Not to me. I never had any trouble with Norman. He's a brilliant lad. A good listener and not a moaner. If he gets dropped, he'll run through brick walls to get back into the side."

Despite having annoyed many of the vast United support by asking for a transfer and with some of the things that appeared in the press, I hoped that I left them on good terms. I think they realise now that it was for the best intentions that I wanted to leave and they know that I always gave them 100 per cent when I pulled on that red jersey. I was later told that the Old Trafford switchboard was jammed solid for two days, as supporters questioned the manager's sanity. Fortunately, Alex Ferguson was not around to take the flak, having headed off to the Far East for United's pre-season friendlies.

Brian Madley (The Sunday People)
"If Norman Whiteside recaptures the form that made him the world's greatest teenager only seven years ago, then Alex Ferguson will have dug his own grave. He'll be pushed in with glee by the whole of the Stretford End."

Tommy Docherty
"I've known Norman since he was thirteen and he was United through and through. There's no way he'd have wanted to leave United unless life was unbearable for him."

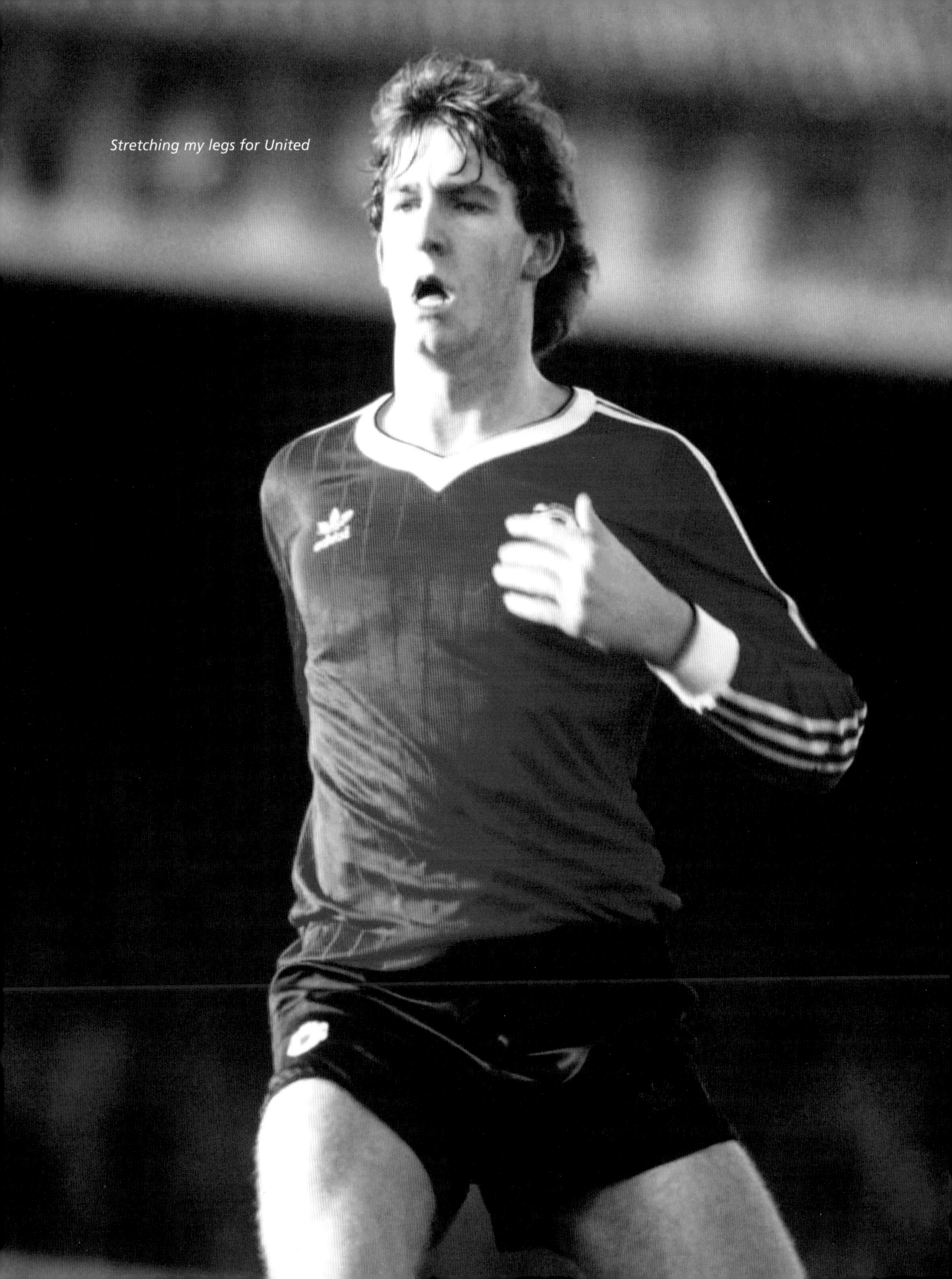

Stretching my legs for United

Sammy McIlroy

"Ferguson has taken the biggest gamble of his life and I can't see why. I've known Norman all his career and I've been with him all over the world with Northern Ireland. He's no troublemaker and if he's overcome his injury problems he still has a great career ahead.

I'd want him in my team instead of playing against me."

"Fergie and I didn't always see eye to eye - but he was always fair with me and I never hid the truth from him"

When I left United, there were so many stories going around that they could have filled this book on their own. Needless to say, none were true.

As I have mentioned previously, I wasn't an angel. Neither was I a player like Ole Gunner Solskjaer or Gary Neville, players who give the manager no sleepless nights, lying awake wondering what they are up to and if he will have to haul them into the office in the morning.

I am also not going to say that Fergie and I always saw eye to eye. But what I will say is, that he was always fair with me and I think that despite the problems I never hid the truth from him.

When I requested a transfer, he knew where I was coming from. In fact, I'm still certain that if he had been in my shoes, he would have done exactly the same thing.

In the confines of his office, he broke the news to me that I was no longer guaranteed a regular first-team place, something that I was already partly aware of. But he then surprised me when he said that Colin Harvey had been in touch and if I was interested then he would telephone him. Before I got the chance to speak to the Everton manager though, he told me what sort of figure I should ask for salary-wise as well as given me other guidelines regarding the transfer.

Thankfully I listened to his advice and upon joining the Goodison Park side, I was suddenly earning more than I had been at United. This was thanks to someone who I was apparently not getting on with.

Perhaps he saw something of himself in me, a lad from a working-class background, who went into every game with the intentions of winning and someone who would go for every ball with the intentions of winning it.

Alex Ferguson is someone for whom I have a lot of respect and I only wish that I could have avoided those injuries that restricted my appearances under him. Perhaps I could have helped bring the Championship to Old Trafford a bit earlier.

When I left United one of the tabloids offered me £50,000 to spill the beans, reveal a few behind closed doors secrets, say what I really thought of Alex Ferguson. You know the sort of thing? Other players had done it, Paul McGrath was one. But, The boss did not go into print with anything about me and I felt that I owed it to him to do likewise. Not that there was anything much to tell.

At the end of the day, Alex Ferguson did what he thought was best for both United and for me.

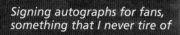

*Signing autographs for fans,
something that I never tire of*

So, I collected my boots and a few other odds and ends, said my goodbyes and drove out of The Cliff training ground for the last time. Within a matter of days, I was meeting up with my new team mates and jetting off to the Far East.

By a strange quirk of fate, my first game in the blue of Everton, eight days after signing, was against my former team mates in the Kobe Stadium Tokyo, where I gave Alex Ferguson one final sleepless night. This time it was not due to any off-the-field antics, but with my contribution on the field over the ninety minutes.

Having played in both midfield and up front for United, I made my Everton debut in the unfamiliar role of sweeper. Colin Harvey's decision to play this system, however, was abandoned at half time, as it was hindering and cramping our style, despite us taking the lead.

We gave United something of a shock after only seventeen minutes, when Tony Cottee opened the scoring. Two minutes later, I beat Mike Duxbury to the ball and opened up the United defence for Neil Pointon to score number two. In the thirty-third minute, I exchanged passes with Cottee and brushed past two defenders to score the third.
United were later to pull one back and the game ended 3-1.

It was certainly not a case of wanting to put one over on United or going out to prove anything or anybody wrong. The whole idea was to get into the groove with my new team mates.

Colin Harvey (Everton manager)
"It was a good performance. I was pleased with Norman. He needs match fitness because he didn't play much last season, but he is doing well."

Unfortunately, my Everton League debut did not get off to such a promising start, as we lost 2-0 at Coventry on the opening day of the season. There was, however, a long campaign ahead and I had a lot of time to make up and I suppose, a lot of people to prove to that I could still play regularly at a high level. One date I had already circled in the diary was September 9th, my first competitive encounter with my old club, when United visited Goodison Park.

I was really looking forward to the game, but I had to treat it as just another fixture. Although, I suppose it wasn't.

The after match headlines in some of the newspapers were slightly embarrassing, with the Daily Telegraph's – 'Ferguson Left To Rue The Day He Sold Whiteside', the Guardian's 'Whiteside The Silent Avenger' and the Manchester Evening News's – 'Whiteside Makes United Faces Red' just three of the many.

Just after half an hour's play, I did what all the United supporters feared I might and that was create a scoring chance, if not for myself then for a team-mate, laying on the first goal. Pouncing on a loose ball on the edge of the United penalty area, I looked up briefly before threading it through to Mike Newell, who shot low past Jim Leighton in the United goal.

Three minutes later, I had the opportunity to put the game even further beyond United's grasp, but my volley, from Newell's pass, went over their crossbar.

Within eight minutes of the second half getting under way, Everton were 3-0 in front and I was once again involved. Just three minutes after the restart I won possession for Kevin Sheedy, who in turn found Pat Nevin, who kept his cool to score

Here I am taking a flying lesson, a career that I didn't persue. It frightened me to death

with ease. Graeme Sharp, diving to head home scored number three, after I had begun the move winning a header in midfield. Shortly afterwards, I was forced to leave the field with a hamstring strain, receiving a standing ovation from the Everton supporters. Don't know if any of the United contingent joined in though!

By a strange coincidence, United began to get a bit more into the game following my departure and in fact scored twice. But with only three minutes to play when they scored the second, Everton managed to hold on to secure the points.

David Hopps (The Guardian)
"On the field he was the avenging angel, with hardly a challenge out of place."

Colin Gibson (The Sunday Telegraph)
"Whiteside was fuelled by the powerful desire to prove United wrong in discarding him at the tender age of 24. He achieved his target with the only flash of enterprise in a fantic first half."

The relief that many within Old Trafford had felt at the departure of Paul McGrath and myself came rebounding back like a bad curry, when Paul accepted the tabloids' cash to spill the beans on life at United. I was happy just to let my feet do the talking, even though I could have made a bit of cash from giving the press a few stories.

At Goodison Park, the Everton support soon took to me, forgetting that I was once a Manchester United player and I was once again enjoying my football, especially as we were playing considerably better than United at this time.
Although struggling in the League, United were progressing in the FA Cup, as were Everton and on the same weekend as United faced Hereford in the fifth round, I was up against my old manager Ron Atkinson, who was now with Sheffield Wednesday. Having already put one over Alex Ferguson, it was as equally pleasing to do the same to Big Ron.

Ron Atkinson
"Why did Fergie sell him? He's buzzing with the old confidence. I am sick that I couldn't afford to buy him when he was available".

A cloud was cast over my promising start with Everton, when I was forced to go into hospital with an Achilles problem, but, much to my relief, I made a quick recovery and was soon adding to my nine goals, with six in seven games. Thankfully I was back in time to make the journey along the East Lancs Road on March 14th to face United at Old Trafford, my first return as an opposition player.

"Having already put one over Alex Ferguson, it was as equally pleasing to do the same to big Ron"

Alex Ferguson
"I bear no ill will for Norman. Any player who achieved what he did for United will always be welcome here. I don't want to go into the reasons behind the decision to sell him. It's a fact of football life these days that very few players stay a lifetime with one club. Norman was a smashing player for us and I hope he continues a successful career with Everton".

As I ran out of the familiar Old Trafford tunnel, I was slightly bewildered and disappointed to be met with an outbreak of booing. Further boos followed seven minutes later, when I upended my old mate Mark Hughes, for which I received a lecture from the referee.

University
College
Salford

Centre for
Health Studies

School of
Podiatry

Back to Uni, starting a new career

The game could have done with a few more lively exchanges, but instead, it petered out to a 0-0 draw, mainly thanks to Neville Southall and by full time, I was treated just the same as any other Everton player.

Shortly before I had made my Old Trafford return, I 'celebrated' a career first. I received my first ever red card, something that would surprise many people! It came, in an FA Cup 5th round replay against Oldham Athletic at Goodison, when the referee adjudged that my challenge on Mike Milligan was rather high.

Despite this, my team-mates held on for a 1-1, draw after extra time, but lost the second replay 2-1. If we had won, who knows what might have been, as Oldham progressed as far as the semi-final stage, where they lost to United in a replay. If we had made it through, I might even have ended Alex Ferguson's Wembley dream, preventing him from winning that so important first trophy and perhaps even getting him the sack that many predicted would have come had he not lifted the cup that season.

By the end of my first season with the Toffees, I was joint top scorer, with fifteen goals to my credit. This was my best ever return since turning professional and perhaps being away from the "under the microscope twenty-four hours a day" existence at Old Trafford helped me relax a little and I didn't have to try extra hard in an effort to please. I could now relax and enjoy my football. The goals were something of a bonus.

I was greatly encouraged by my first year at Goodison Park and certainly looked forward to season 1990-91, as I felt that things could only get better. How wrong could I be?

During a practise match at Everton's training ground on September 20th, a date I will never forget, I was tackled from behind by one of the junior players. I went down on my knee and it hurt like hell. I was in terrible pain. Having already had eight knee operations, I am surprised that there was still anything there to give me any pain, but there was and it did.

Off I went to see a surgeon and it did not take him long to give his verdict. "You'll spend the rest of your life in a wheel-chair if you keep on playing" he announced and that was basically that. I had only played thirteen League games for Everton this season.

Steve Bates (The Sunday People)
"I can reveal that Norman Whiteside met the Players Union boss Gordon Taylor a week ago for almost three hours. He wanted clarification of the procedure when a player has to finish through injury and the financial package that he could expect. An Everton source told me last night: "Yes its true, there is a deep concern for Norman's future. A final decision, though, is down to Norman and nobody's rushing him."

I did give it some consideration throughout the rest of season 1990-91, as I recovered from yet another operation. I knew what the answer would have to be, but I just did not want to admit it.

The players at other league club's scattered around the country had still to report back for pre-season training, but instead of being one of the many, wondering if I would be over-weight, if I would find the first few days harder than before or whatever, I was contemplating my future outside the game. June hadn't even rolled into July and here I was announcing that despite endless specialist help, I was having to terminate my contract with Everton.

At the age of twenty-six, my playing days were over and the hard man shed a few tears when the realisation first set in. I felt nothing but emptiness. I was unemployed, with nothing to fall back on. Perhaps if it had happened four or five years down the line then I might have had something that I could move into, but it wasn't the future, it was now and I had nothing.

So, what was I going to do?

I had spent long periods of my career on the treatment tables, especially at United and during those long drawn out days at Old Trafford under the capable hands of Jimmy McGregor. In an effort to pass the time, the United physiotherapist would teach me all about the different muscles, which I would memorise and he would in turn ask me questions about them. I was in the treatment room so often, I practically knew it better than my own living room at home.

"The Stretford End was packed, as it was the last match before it was to be demolished "

Having known nothing else but a life in football, I decided that I would like to remain in the game in some capacity, with a career in physiotherapy my new aim. That meant going back to school, or schools as it turned out, with a course in Health Studies at Stockport College and a Physics GCSE at North Trafford. Never having studied before, it was a testing time.

Practise makes perfect they say, so I was more than grateful to my old Northern Ireland team-mate Sammy McIlroy, who had begun season 1991-92 in charge of Northwich Victoria. Out of the blue, Sammy invited me to help him look after the players as a trainee physiotherapist.

Despite my career with Manchester United sailing along on stormy waters at times, I was more than delighted when the directors agreed to allow a testimonial match for me to be played at Old Trafford. As the date, May 3rd 1992, drew closer, I spent a lot of the time walking around with my fingers crossed, but for nothing concerning the match itself.

United, were still chasing that elusive Championship and by the end of April trailed Leeds United by one point. They had three games remaining to Leeds' two, so could they clinch the long awaited title and parade the trophy around Old Trafford on my big day?

As it turned out, consecutive defeats against Liverpool and West Ham United handed the title to arch-rivals Leeds, taking much of the shine off my testimonial match and only 7,434 turned up to watch Everton run out 4-2 winners. United were at one stage 2-0 in front, but Everton turned the momentum up in the second half

Certainly, the attendance was disappointing, but the Stretford End was packed, many though were perhaps there more to say farewell to the famous old section of the ground than for my benefit, as it was the last match when supporters could stand on that particular terracing before it was demolished to be replaced by a stand.

In the end, the physiotherapy idea fell through, as I didn't have enough qualifications, so I set off for school again. This time I gained all my GCSE's and A levels and then decided to take a podiatry course. Well, I'd knackered that many feet during my playing career I thought I could perhaps put something back and mend a few!

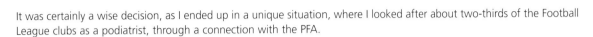

It was certainly a wise decision, as I ended up in a unique situation, where I looked after about two-thirds of the Football League clubs as a podiatrist, through a connection with the PFA.

I also returned to Old Trafford doing match-day corporate hospitality, along with the likes of Stuart Pearson and Wilf McGuinness. Generally, we just go around the various suites or whatever, cracking a few jokes and telling a few stories to keep the punters happy.

It is great to be back at United on match days, especially as it coincides with such brilliant times for the club. You feel that you are actually part of it all.

> ## "I had a few good years at the top
> ## and achieved a couple of things that the likes of
> ## George Best never managed to do"

Occasionally, I bump into Sir Alex and we'll stop for a chat, something that many might find surprising, as there are people out there who believe that we just don't see eye to eye, or haven't done so in the past. I remember walking down one of the corridors after the Championship win of 2001 and I saw him celebrating with his family and friends. Next thing I knew, he has dragged me in, stuck a bottle of champagne into my hand and told me to "get it down my neck". I was also invited to his testimonial dinner at the G-Mex as one of the VIP guests. Who says that we don't get on?

Over the years, I have often been asked if I have any regrets or if I had my time again would I do things differently? What has happened has happened and I would do most of it again. Perhaps though with the stricter diets and whatever today, I might have benefited from a few things.

As for regrets? Obviously, the injuries, but I had a few good years at the top. I played in the World Cup and scored the winning goal in an FA Cup Final, two things that George Best never managed to do.

No, I've had my time, did the above and most of all, I played for the biggest and the best club in the world – Manchester United.

My '85 boots, well worn and battered.
Hung up prematurely

Chapter 12

MAN UTD & NORTHERN IRELAND RECORD

Name: Norman Whiteside
Born: May 7th 1965 in Belfast

Manchester United
Signed as associated shoolboy, September 1978
Signed as apprentice, June 1981
Signed as professional, July 1982

Debut:	Brighton & Hove Albion v **Manchester United.** April 24th 1982 (as substitute)
Full Debut:	**Manchester United** v Stoke City. May 15th 1982
First Senior Goal:	**Manchester United** v Stoke City. May 15th 1982

Playing Record	Season	Appearances	Goals
Football League	1981-82	1 (1 sub)	1
	1982-83	39	8
	1983-84	30 (7 sub)	10
	1984-85	23 (4 sub)	9
	1985-86	37	4
	1986-87	31	8
	1987-88	26 (1 sub)	7
	1988-89	6	0
	Total	193 (13 sub)	47
F.A. Cup	1982-83	7	3
	1983-84	1	0
	1984-85	6	4
	1985-86	5	1
	1986-87	2	1
	1987-88	3	1
	Total	24	10
Football League Cup	1982-83	7 (2 sub)	3
	1983-84	6	1
	1984-85	1	0
	1985-86	4	2
	1986-87	3 (1sub)	1
	1987-88	5	2
	Total	26 (3 sub)	9
UEFA Cup	1982-83	2	0
	1984-85	4	0
ECW Cup	1983-84	5 (1 sub)	1
	Total	11 (1 sub)	1
Northern Ireland	Total	36 full caps (1 Under 23 cap) (2 additional when playing for Everton)	9